MOSAICS FROM INDIA

VIEW OF AGRA CITY.—See Page 221.

Mosaics From India

TALKS ABOUT INDIA, ITS PEOPLES, RELIGIONS AND CUSTOMS

BY

MARGARET BOEHME DENNING

MUZAFFARPUR, INDIA

Fleming H. Revell Company

Chicago : New York : Toronto

MCMII

CONTENTS.

LIST OF ILLUSTRATIONS

INTRODUCTION

Wander with me through Hindustan—the land of varied peoples, tongues and climes, of romance and of poetry, and yet the land of sorrow, poverty and false gods.

We shall wish to see old temples, wherein, since long ago, these peoples have searched after God, drifting into strange, idolatrous worship, not finding the Living One. Here and there we shall listen to talks by the wayside, in out-caste huts or in curtained zenanas. We shall go out into the beautiful country and, standing beside Mother Ganges, see the trees so rich in blossom, delight our eyes with the beauty of old palaces and visit tombs and mosques. Yet, most of all, we shall hope to get near the people at their vocations, in their ceremonies and in their worship— near to the heart of India. And, as we see and know these people better, knowledge will inspire pity, then sympathy, sometimes admiration, and all will give place to *love*. They will be no longer barbarians, but simply strayed brothers of our common family. And, having learned to love them, we must long to bring them home to the family reunion, for "Love never faileth."

Some chapters of this book have appeared in "The Chautauquan," "The Missionary Review of the World" and other publications, and I am greatly indebted to their publishers for permission to reprint. Monier Williams' book on "Brahminism" has been consulted on points regarding caste and customs.

CHAPTER I.

BOMBAY.

From the sea, Bombay is imposing. The towers and fine buildings near Apollo Bunder, or Prince's Dock, look fair in the Indian sunshine, and a closer view of the part known as "The Fort" confirms the impression. The city, almost free from smoke, retains in its buildings the beauty of variously tinted stone. The Esplanade is a beautiful sight, indeed, with its fine Elphinstone College and the many other stone buildings along its length. Malabar Hill, also, with its trees, gardens and elegant residences, is an enticing part of the city. "Victoria Terminus" is the finest railway station in the world. Everything in this European Bombay conveys the idea of space, verdure, comfort and wealth. Fine equipages roll along the wide streets in the late afternoons and in the golden evenings of a climate of perpetual summer; beautiful Parsee ladies in dainty, silken, flowing attire, flit by among English beauties, while now and then a darker-hued but attractive Marathi face may be seen. Native gentlemen in rich and becoming headgear known as a "pugri," drive everywhere, and the Parsee's peculiar "stove-pipe," without a brim, is omnipresent. On the streets a throng, more truly cosmopolitan than is found anywhere else, sweeps along or

13

turns aside to enjoy the cool of the evening in little parks or along the sea-beach.

All this brightness, movement and beauty, belong to *European* Bombay, although many of the wealthy and high-caste people share in it also. The native city is very different. Here are the narrow, badly drained streets, the crowded tenements, where the plague finds such congenial quarters, and the numberless small shops which delight the foreigner and reward the curio-seeking tourist. In this part of Bombay the habits and customs of the people may be studied, as life is studied in crowded Naples. However, here in the oriental city one notes a remarkable absence of the feminine element of the city's life. The few women seen belong to the lower classes, with the exception of the favored high-born Marathi woman, who need not go veiled, or the fair Parsee lady, who rivals her Western sister in freedom as well as in beauty.

All sorts of occupations are carried on out-of-doors—not only the trades and handicrafts, but household duties as well. Here are fruits or grain being laid out in the sun to dry, a baby enjoying its bath on a door-step, rice in process of cleaning, a barber busy on the curbstone, a woman scouring brass cooking-pots—and all in the teeming streets of Bombay. The same unconcern regarding outward appearances will be found all over India. As the coolies work on the roads, pounding in sandstone and concrete, they sing in concert, or, in responsive couplets, keep time with their *doolmuts*, or pounders. Processions of all sorts pass through the streets, singing wedding ditties, funeral dirges or religious chants. Wedding dinners are served on the road in front of the bride's or bridegroom's house, and the guests seem to enjoy the feast all the more for being the cynosures of hungry eyes. Almost hide-bound by caste-rules and observances, the people of India are nevertheless free as air from the restrictions of our so-called proprieties.

This out-door life is, in certain phases, very attractive and delightful, suited to the people and to the climate and fascinating to the foreigner from colder lands; but it is also pathetic in many ways. Its saddest feature is the dearth of real family-life, the absence of the home. Men may sit in groups and smoke or dally over their sherbet, but no family group is ever visible, except among the Parsees or resident foreigners. Even the Marathi woman, though not hid away as are most high-caste women, is never seen with her husband and sons. Traveling about India one misses more and more the shut-in millions—the lonely women for whom the marvelous Eastern moonlight means but a few rays in a dingy, walled back-yard, and for whom the flowers and groves bloom and blossom in vain.

The great diversity of vehicles and animals in Bombay is very interesting. Almost all sorts of English carriages are used. Then there is the huge bullock-coach, holding eight or ten, drawn by the fine, humped Indian ox, and the queer little top-heavy *ekka,* meant for one only, as its name signifies, but often fairly bulging with its human freight. Among the fine English turnouts, the country carts, the bullock-

coaches and the horsecars, may be seen also the un-
gainly black buffaloes, dragging heavy drays slowly
along, and all combining to make a medley of traffic
unknown in any but an Indian city. The horses belonging to the streetcars usually wear white sun-hats
tied down under their chins in a most comical, grand-
motherly style.

Besides these sights there are the Chinese shops,
the queer little places where one can buy curios; the
wonderful Crawford Market with its unrivaled fruit,
the mango, and an almost endless variety of other
fruits. But to one who loves his race, the most interesting, yet most pathetic, of all this city's varied
spectacles is her teeming millions. The newcomer is
always shocked by the prevalent semi and total nakedness seen here. Even those not limited by poverty to
a narrow loin-cloth, by preference often wear nothing
else. This custom, universal among the lower
classes, extends to the higher orders when sitting in
the doorways of their homes or in their shops.

Altogether, Bombay belongs to a strange new
world, yet an old, old, slowly changing world—the
Orient, which fascinates while it repels.

THE SOROSIS CLUB AT BOMBAY.

Upon invitation of Dr. Emma Ryder, the President
of the Sorosis Club of Bombay, I drove one afternoon
down the Esplanade to the Girls' School, where an
"at home" of the club was given in honor of the
Governor's wife.

At the gate of the compound, or yard, my husband left me and I ascended the stairs alone, for gentlemen were not permitted on the second landing even, as many ladies had accepted the invitation of Dr. Ryder on condition and promise that gentlemen were not to be present.

It was a brilliant scene. The room was large and airy, with many doors and windows opening upon verandas on either side. At one end of the room, partly hidden by curtains and a screen, was a table spread with dainties new and rare to Western eyes. Fine palms in huge pots adorned the archways, and tasteful articles of Indian bric-à-brac were used in profusion.

The company could well be called "exclusive," for we were admitted behind the Mohammedan *purdahs* and enjoyed associations which a few years ago would have been denied to all. There were present representatives of at least six nationalities and of almost as many religions. A few of the company were American and English ladies, some Mohammedan and Hindu, but the larger number were Parsees. This was owing in part to the proximity of the Parsee Girls' School and also to the fact that some of the young ladies from the school were to take part in the program.

A more richly dressed assembly it would be difficult to find; yet not a single specimen of the so-called "full-dress" costume was there. The Hindu women were attired in a tasteful and costly manner, but their garments were of sober hues. Their head-ornaments of gold were massive and beautiful, the hair being drawn smoothly back into a knot and fastened by these gold medallions. The Mohammedans wore rich costumes and fine ornaments and were distinguished by embroidered turbans; but the brilliancy and light of the company came from the soft and shimmering silks of the Parsee ladies—white, rich red, peach, pink, blue, pale yellows and lovely tints of light green blending and mingling in kaleidoscopic fashion. These graceful garments were trimmed with gold and silver braid, rich lace and bands of embroidered ribbon. The necklaces, bracelets, and, in the case of the Hindus, the nose-jewels and anklets, made a soft, tinkling noise as their owners moved about. It was an Arabian Nights scene. Yet this very tinkling of the wristlets and anklets sounded to me like the noise of chains, for, as I looked into the beautiful faces, I thought that the shadows of oppression were there.

But what is the Sorosis and what are its objects? It is, in brief, the daughter of the New York Sorosis, a club which was organized for purely literary purposes and aimed at a confederation of many similar clubs.

When Dr. Ryder arrived in India she was wonderfully impressed with the narrowness of the lives lived by even the most favored of India's women. Family weddings, births and deaths—and for the rest the merest trifles—made up the sum total of their experience. History, deeds of heroism and the vivid life of to-day seemed scarcely to reach them at all. Mrs. Ryder felt it her plain duty to open the world in some

way to these women. The first step in this direction
was the insertion of a notice in the Bombay papers to
the effect that, on a certain Saturday afternoon, she
would be glad to receive all women who would come,
with a view to forming a woman's club.

Great apprehension was felt by Mrs. Ryder's
friends as to the outcome of this experiment. They
were sure it would either end in failure or in the
gathering together of a very doubtful company. However, the day arrived, and with it forty women of
various creeds and nationalities. A club was formed
and christened "Sorosis."

A reading-room forms the center of attraction for
the club. To this women may come who never before
ventured anywhere alone. To many it is the only
thing of interest outside of their homes. Here are
choice books and magazines and here these women
come to discuss all sorts of topics, or to fraternize in
a manner previously unheard of in this land of caste
and social barriers.

Here the Hindu meets the Parsee and both meet
the Christian, whether European, Eurasian, or native.
Strangest of all, the seclusive, shrouded Mussulmani
steals in, and, unveiling, takes her share in the new
comradeship.

There are regular fortnightly meetings and an occasional "at home," or tea. At every regular meeting
a twenty-minute lecture is given on the life of some
worthily distinguished woman. Elizabeth Fry, Miss
Carpenter, Frances Willard and others have, in this
way, been infusing new aspirations and thoughts into

the minds and hearts of these Eastern sisters. Essays
are read and music is rendered in Persian, English,
Marathi and Arabic. As will be seen, some of these
women know something of certain branches of education, but their lives are shut in and narrow. The club
gives them some opportunity to exercise their mental
muscle and to belong, in a measure, to the age in which
they live.

There is no missionary work connected with this
movement; but, although we may depreciate the presence of an idol on the piano, even though it be merely
for ornament, and may wish there were a more distinct-
ly Christian atmosphere in these gatherings, still a
good work is being done in the opening of hitherto
closed doors and in the burning away of caste-barriers
in the fires of social life and kindred interests.

Over the door of the room is the motto sent to Dr.
Ryder by the President of the New York Sorosis:
"Tell them the world was made for women also."
Strange new doctrine for India! Yet in the gatherings in the mission schools for girls all over the empire, in the passage of the "Bill of Consent" and in
Pandita Ramabai's School for Widows in Poona—in
all these we see the dawn of hope for India's womanhood.

Some day meetings such as I have described will
not be so rare. Pandita's school will not be the "lone
star" of hope for twenty-one million widows. Some
day this beautiful Eastern world will indeed be made
for women also, for some day our God will rule in this
land of the palm and citron, and King Emmanuel will

be the Lord. Then infants will not be married, nor child-widows cry by reason of their bitter bondage. Then will the Sun of Righteousness arise with healing in His wings, and there shall be "no more curse" upon the women and the homes of India.

"TOWERS OF SILENCE."

One of the most weirdly interesting scenes in Bombay is the place where the Parsees dispose of their dead, known as the "Towers of Silence." One day, in company with an American lady, we drove over beautiful Malabar Hill to this strange spot. As it stands on an eminence overlooking the sea, protected on the landward side by a high stone wall, we could see nothing of the towers as we approached. We alighted at the gate and were admitted by the dignified gate-keeper. Another Parsee showed us over the grounds, which are carefully laid out in gravel walks and dotted with various kinds of palms, the variegated crotons, often called "the flowers of India," and with many flowering trees. From these trees and plants each visitor received a bouquet on leaving.

Here and there are several temples dedicated to fire-worship, the religion of the Parsees. Five priests keep the fire burning continuously in these temples, and, since the first Persians landed in Bombay, over two hundred years ago, this fire has never been allowed to go out. The trees, parterres of flowers, the neat walks and even the fire-temples were pleasant to the eye—but these were not what we had come to see.

All these are merely the setting for the five round towers of white masonry, scattered here and there among the shrubbery. These are the "Towers of Silence," where the Parsees expose their dead to be devoured by vultures.

Those grewsome objects perched in an unbroken row upon the edges of every parapet are motionless birds awaiting their ghoulish feast. One of these solid white towers, with its fringe of black vultures standing out in relief against the sky, is a sickening sight; for the disposal of the dead by exposing their bodies to these loathsome birds is certainly the most revolting of all the methods of disposing of lifeless clay.

The towers are open to the sky above, but all the interior is hidden from sight by outer walls, rising fourteen feet above the stone platform on which the dead are laid. They are perhaps thirty feet high and ninety feet in diameter.

Although no one has ever seen the interior except the builders and those who carry the dead to the towers, there is a large model about three feet in diameter, kept locked in a wooden box near the gate, which the guide will exhibit and explain, and by means of which a fair idea of the whole structure may be obtained. This model, and one exactly similar, which was sent to the Paris Exposition, are the only ones ever made, the old Parsee told us. We have since been informed that miniature ones are for sale in Bombay. However this may be, we have never been able to secure one as a curio.

The plan of a tower is approximately this: a cir-

cular platform, fourteen feet below the topmost level
of the outer wall, and, as already described, open to
sun, wind and rain, receives the bodies. This platform
is divided into three concentric rings of stone receptacles. The outer row is for men, the middle for
women and the inner for children. In the center, oc-
cupying the greater part of the tower, is the well.

These receptacles are connected by gutters, cut between them, and the rains wash away all uncleanness
from the bodies, which have been stripped of flesh by
the birds of prey. This water passes into the great
well, where it percolates through the bleaching bones
of thousands of Parsees, and from thence is carried off
through huge underground drains. There are four of
these drains, and at the entrance of every one is a large
box of charcoal intended to purify the water before it
is discharged into the earth. There are, perhaps,
methods of renewing this charcoal when it becomes
clogged with impurities. On a level with the platform
is a door reached from the ground by an inclined plane
of stonework, by which the bearers enter with the body
of the dead. Having placed their burden in one of the
receptacles, they hasten out, when, from a position in
the garden, the black fringe will be seen to disappear
from the top of the tower. The vultures are feeding!
Perchance on the body of a sweet, beautiful child, but
lately held in a mother's loving embrace. No one may
witness them at their revolting feast; but presently
they return, satisfied, to the parapet or to a perch among
the trees. Two weeks after the burial the bearers return and, with a pair of long tongs, throw the bones

into the great well. The clothes in which the dead were wrapped, as well as those worn by the bearers, are all left inside the garden in a small stone house, where they are burned. Every time the bearers carry a body to the towers they are provided with new, pure, white garments by the friends of the deceased. These bearers, who prepare the dead and carry them into the regions of silence, must live separate from the Parsee community, as they are considered unclean, and, in order to induce anyone to embrace this vocation, the pay for the service is placed very high.

The reason given for this strange disposition of the dead is this: to hasten the return of the body to the original elements worshiped by the Parsees—earth, air, water and fire—and to maintain the greatest possible purity.

One wonders, however, at this explanation, for the Hindu method of burning-ghäts is a far speedier, simpler and less repulsive method of accomplishing the same result.

There are many strange stories and traditions connected with these towers. It is even said that if by mistake a living man should be carried there in a faint or swoon, and should reach the interior, he would not be carried back, even were he to revive, but the door would be closed and the unfortunate left to his fate. Whether this is true or not, it is scarcely more tragic than the sight, often witnessed in Bombay, of a funeral procession being met on the way to the gardens by a flock of hungry vultures which have been waiting some days for a meal.

No one is allowed within this enclosure except a Parsee—so the sign board said. But, like many other rules, this was made null and void by the jingle of a little silver. The other rule, which prohibits anyone but a bearer of the dead from approaching within thirty feet of a tower, was, however, rigidly enforced.

The masonry of the towers is massive. The first one was built two hundred years ago, when the Parsees first came to Bombay. This oldest one is only used at present by the Modi family of Bombay. The last one of the five was erected forty-five years ago. There is a sixth tower, a square one, standing by itself in the garden, where rest the bones of the criminals of the Parsee community.

We took the flowers from the old Parsee as a souvenir of our visit, and turned from the beautiful grounds and white towers with their ornaments of living bronze. As we drove along the shores of the back bay toward home, we mused thankfully on our Christian burial rite, and Longfellow's beautiful couplet came to mind—

> Lay him who loved Mother Nature,
> Softly to sleep on her breast.

And the scenes in "Sweet Auburn," across the seas, in all their naturalness and beauty, seemed a fitting foil to this spectacle of mystery in the cemetery of the fire-worshipers of Bombay.

CHAPTER II.

THE GOVERNMENT OF INDIA.

India is ruled by the British. King Edward VII., sitting upon his throne in London, is the Mähäräjäh of the Land of the Vedas, and the Anglo-Saxon mind has greatly changed the complexion and modified the thought of that oriental country.

The people of India are not one, but many peoples. The three hundred million inhabitants of that sunny land include representatives of several races of men, whose complexions range from pure white, through golden brown to black, with mental culture of all grades, from that slightly above the animal to the learned doctors of philosophy or of law. The Maratha and the Madrasi, the Parsee and the Panjabi, the Bengali and the Bhil, the Gond and the Gurkha, are samples of the variety of types represented. Besides, there are the foreigners; some of them temporary sojourners, others who have permanently settled in the land. Passing through the streets of Bombay or Calcutta one meets with almost every nationality that the sun shines upon. The Englishman, of course, is very prominent. Every other nation of Europe is represented. The American is there, too, and the Japanese, the Arab, the African, West Indian, Chinaman, and even the Fiji islanders. But the masses of people met with are East Indians, or natives of the land, who differ as widely one from another as the foreigners themselves.

Another element in this population is the Eurasian —a mixture of European and Asiatic blood, representing every degree of intermingling, from almost pure English to the almost pure native. This class numbers a hundred thousand souls. They almost invariably adopt the customs of the Europeans and many of them are highly cultured and refined.

The religions of India separate its people still more widely than race characteristics. Some worship idols, back of which are all sorts of imaginary spirits, good and evil—mostly the latter; others worship themselves, or one another. Some worship the devil outright, while others lift up their hands and hearts in adoration of the true God who made the heavens and the earth. Over this mixed multitude the British flag waves and the British Räj (Government) is supreme.

The early history of India is little known. The Hindu despises history. Not one in a hundred knows the date of his birth or of the birth of his child. The origin of the human race or of the Hindu people, or the date of his sacred books, is as far back as the strength of his imagination will carry it. In the record of national events fiction plays a larger part than fact. But from the Aryan invasion, about 1500 B. C., India has seen the rise and fall of many governments. The Aryans conquered the aboriginal tribes, but they themselves became divided into petty kingdoms. Sometimes one prince stronger than the rest would prevail over his neighbors and add their territory to his own; but after his death his successors would lose the advantage that he had gained.

About the eleventh century of our era the Mohammedans gained a footing in the Punjab. They were engaged in many wars, and the rule that they established was alternately strong and weak, the extent of their territory varying with the power of their chief ruler. In the sixteenth and seventeenth centuries the Mohammedan authority reached its climax in the Mogul Dynasty. The Taj Mahal and the forts at Agra and Delhi are monuments to the splendor of that Mogul age.

When the English first went to India, in the sixteenth century, their only motive was commercial. They had seen the ships of the Portuguese and the Dutch return from the East laden with spices, ivory, pearl and other rich treasures, and they, too, wished to share in this trade. Several English merchants ventured out, each on his own responsibility. But a six-months' voyage around the Cape of Good Hope, with a return journey of equal length, made, too, in boats much less able to weather the storms of the sea than the huge vessels of the present day, rendered individual enterprize hazardous. The trading companies of Portugal and Holland were under the patronage of their governments. At that time it was the popular idea that the sovereign should be the patron of the trades of his subjects. There had been an effort for several years in England to form a company for trading in the East Indias, but the uncertainty of its being profitable made capitalists hesitate. Finally a company was organized to which, in the year 1600, a royal charter was granted by Queen Elizabeth. This is popularly known as the East India Company and was given the monopoly of the English trade beyond the Cape of Good Hope and the Straits of Magellan.

At first this company made voyages to India, taking goods and money from England and exchanging them for commodities saleable in the homeland. As their business increased they began to acquire grants of land in India and to construct factories. Since these properties must be protected, a police force was added, then a standing army. At that time there were many petty kingdoms in India and many chiefs who were frequently at war with one another. The British, with their wealth and their standing army, constituted a sort of neutral power. It often happened that a native prince who was being overpowered in war would appeal to the Company for aid, and in return would grant it concessions of land and special trading privileges in his territory. As these territorial possessions and the influence of the company increased it gradually became a power to be reckoned with in the political affairs of India. One kingdom after another fell into its hands until the power of the company became the greatest in India. The East India Company, being a private enterprise, the government received no share in its profits, although large loans were often made by it to Parliament in cases of necessity. It was of the nature of a limited trust company, dependent upon Parliament for its authority.

Its charter was modified from time to time, to suit new conditions, and the legislation of Parliament concerning it was adapted to its growth until it finally became a sort of provincial government for India.

This was the state of things when the great Indian Mutiny occurred in 1857. After the mutiny, in the year 1858, the English government assumed direct control of British India. Queen Victoria added to her title the phrase, "Empress of India," and the British East India Company ceased to exist.

At the present time nearly all India is under the British crown, the only exceptions being a small possession still retained by the French in the south, a little strip on the west coast belonging to Portugal, and three native states—Nepal, Sikkim and Bhutan— which are independent.

British rule is of two kinds: 1 Direct. 2 Protectorate over native states. There are still many states that are under the supervision of the British, but whose territory has not yet come into their actual possession. These states are allowed a measure of independence and are permitted to govern themselves under prescribed limitations. In all cases their princes and chiefs are bound by treaty engagements acknowledging British supremacy and surrendering all right to make war or peace, to open diplomatic relations with neighbors or foreigners, to maintain armies above a certain strength, or to offer hospitality to Europeans other than those agreeable to the Governor General. In all cases the treaties give power to the British to depose the native ruler in case of mismanagement. At the court of each important prince lives a British Resident appointed by the Governor General, whose approval must be given to all the laws enacted by the native prince or his council before they can go into effect.

About one-fourth of British India is included in these native protected domains. A hundred or more of them are large enough to be called states, but many more are mere chieftainships. The most important is Hyderabad, in the south central part of India, which includes a population of ten million, over against others which number but a few thousand each. The other three-fourths of the country is ruled by the English directly.

The King of England is the ultimate authority in British India. He appoints a Secretary of State for India, who is the practical head of affairs, is a member of the King's Cabinet by virtue of his office and resides in England. He is assisted by a council of from ten to fifteen members, appointed by himself from among distinguished persons who have lived in India and are acquainted with the country. The members of this council live in England and constitute a sort of advisory committee without ultimate authority. To the Secretary and this council of his appointing is intrusted the conduct of all the business transacted in the United Kingdom in relation to the government of India. The House of Commons has too much to do in other matters to occupy its time and attention in the minutiæ of the Indian government. Hence it entrusts to the Secretary, assisted by his advisers, all affairs pertaining to the Eastern Empire. The House frequently discusses the actions of the Secretary of State for India, and expresses its approval or disapproval, but seldom interferes directly.

In India the executive authority is vested in a Governor General, popularly known as Viceroy. He is appointed by the King, but is under the direction of the Secretary of State for India. He is assisted by an Executive Council, consisting of six ordinary members appointed by the crown, and from six to twelve additional members appointed by the Governor General. The commander-in-chief of the army in India is also a member of this council. The various departments of state, as finance, public works, home affairs, military works, are each presided over by an ordinary member, and the secretaries of each department look to him for orders. The portfolio of Foreign Affairs is usually held by the Governor General himself, with the aid of the secretaries and attaches of the Foreign Office. The Governor General, in council, under the sanction of the Secretary of State for India, has power to make laws for all British India. For political purposes the territory is divided into provinces, with a chief executive officer for each. Two of these provinces, Bombay and Madras, are called presidencies, because they were formerly governed by a president and council. Their chief executives are called governors, and are appointed by the Crown. The heads of the other provinces are called either Lieutenant-governors or Chief Commissioners, and are appointed by the Governor General. The Governors of Bombay and

Madras are assisted by executive and legislative coun-
cils. The Lieutenant-Governor of Bengal has a legislative council. These provincial governments are
related to the central government of India, as the several states in America are related to the government at
Washington, though the monarchical idea that prevails
among the British makes the form of government very
different.

Each province is divided into districts, or counties.
These vary in size, and their boundaries are frequently
determined by rivers, hills, mountain ranges or other
landmarks. The district is really the fundamental unit
of administration. Its chief officer is called "collector"
or "deputy commissioner." The collector is a magistrate and has a wide scope of magisterial power, dif-
fering in the various provinces. He is also the chief
land-revenue officer of the district. He is usually
called by the natives *Bara Sahib* (big master) or some
similar title, and to those not knowing from whence his
power comes he seems a little king in his own territory. Viewed from the standpoint of the central government of the province, however, he is simply an executive officer under very minute regulations. He has
a number of assistants, usually natives, whose number
varies according to the size and importance of the district. Some are magistrates with powers in civil or
criminal cases; others are revenue officers who, in the
north, are called *tahsildars,* a *tahsil* meaning "A place
of collecting." There are also "assistant," or *"naib
tahsildars."* These again have assistants, as revenue
inspectors, patwäris, and the like.

Several districts are grouped together in a "division," and each division has its commissioner. This officer ranks between the district officer and the chief commissioner, and is a very important factor in the government.

In the judicial department also the system is complete. Each of the provinces of Bombay, Bengal, Madras and Northwest Provinces has a High Court. In the other provinces one or more judicial commissioners are the highest judicial authority. There are also civil and criminal courts descending to that of the *munsif,* or squire.

In the constabulary each district has its district superintendent of police, who has under him inspectors, sub-inspectors, constables and patrolmen. Each province has an inspector-general of police, who is at the head of the provincial force.

A system somewhat similar prevails in the medical and educational departments. Each district is supplied with one or more civil surgeons and inspectors of education. These again are under the direction of their provincial officers. Besides these are the postal, excise, engineering, forest and other departments, each graded to suit its own requirements, and with each officer's authority and duties specifically marked out.

The great majority of the higher officers of government are Englishmen. The civil service (including such officers as collectors, or deputy commissioners, who may rise to be commissioners, chief commissioners, lieutenant-governors and the like) is now entered by competitive examinations. A yearly exam-

ination is held in England. The name of each candidate is presented to a special committee. If, after careful investigation, his health, moral character and probable fitness are approved, he is permitted to sit for examination. The list of subjects upon which he may be examined is a long one, some compulsory and some optional, and opposite each subject is the number of possible marks allowed to each. The candidates receiving the greatest number of marks are chosen to the Indian Civil Service in numbers proportional to the requirements of the service for the year. These examinations are now open to a limited number of native gentlemen, also, who go to England to prepare for it. After the successful candidates have received their appointments they still have annual examinations for several years on law, vernacular language and the like.

Candidates for other departments of the government service must pass examinations in their several departments, though less severe than those for the civil service.

The British endeavor to give the people of India a share in their own government; thus, as just mentioned, a limited number of native gentlemen is permitted to compete for the civil service. Some of them become "additional" members of the Governor General's council; some judges in the High Courts; others deputy postmasters general, deputy inspectors of education, subordinate judges, while hundreds of the minor offices are open to them. In most places the Municipal Council (Board of Aldermen) is almost

wholly composed of native gentlemen, some appointed
by the Collector, and the rest elected by qualified voters
of the community. They have power to act upon
measures presented to them by the district officer and
also to enact laws, subject to his approval.

To govern India is not an easy task. There are
local conditions that must be taken into account. Many
of the old customs of the Hindus and Mohammedans
that have come down from ancient time must be respected so far as is consistent with good, stable, moral
government. The English endeavor to accommodate
themselves to these conditions. The laws of marriage,
of inheritance, of adoption, of partition of property,
that have obtained for many centuries, remain to-day
with but little change. There is also the great system
of caste among the Hindus. Each caste has its own
rules in regard to eating and drinking, marriage, and
the observance of religious rites, with its own committee, or *Panchäyat,* in every village or ward of a
city. The *Panchäyat* sits in judgment upon its members on all points pertaining to caste-rules and on many
points of moral conduct. Usually the punishments
decreed for disobedience to caste-rules are recognized
and enforced by the government, unless the culprit
wishes to forsake his caste completely, in which case he
is at liberty to do so.

The great variety of religions in India also makes
the problem of government difficult. The many Hindu
religions all have some things in common, but many
divergences. Kali worship prevails in one place;
Mahä Dev in another; Ganpati in a third. The Jains

have a modified Buddhism, and they, too, are divided
into sects. The various reform movements—as Arya
Samäj, Brahmo Samäj, Prathna Samäj—differ
greatly. The Mohammedan sects worship God according to the teachings of the Arabian prophet, de-
spising idol-worship as sincerely as the Christian. The
Parsees reverence fire, water, earth and air. The government must, if possible, be so administered as not to
disturb the religious sentiments of this variety of people.

The diversity of languages in India tends to separate its people. There are more than threescore
of independent languages, each prevailing in its own
territory, besides many dialects so distinct as often to
be called separate languages. The collector familiar
with the speech and customs of the Marathis of Bombay may not know a word of Tamil of South India.
These people belong to two different races.

Added to these differences are the climatic varia-
tions. The northern and southern extremities of the
territory are separated by twenty-nine degrees of lati-
tude. The characteristics and occupations of the peoples in the various zones within these limits present
great dissimilarities. In the south the heat is *perennial,*
modified on either coast by the oceans adjoining. In
the north there is intense heat in the summer, with
occasional snows in winter and one monsoon (rainy
season) lasting from June to October. There is little
or no rain from October to June. In the south there
are two monsoons, making the conditions of life unlike those in the north.

Another difficulty in the path of the government is the untrustworthiness of the people themselves. Honesty and integrity are not at par in India. When the farmer sows his seed he must begin at once to watch his field, otherwise his neighbor would inspect it during the night, bringing his cattle with him, and in the morning the growing blades would be eaten off level with the ground. The growing grain would all be stolen if the farmer was not on the alert. In harvest-time the reapers must be searched every evening to make sure that their pockets and shirts are not hiding grain. When the crop is on the threshing-floor the farmer, or one or more of his immediate family, must be there day and night to prevent its being carried off. A servant left in charge would probably sell a large portion of it and forget to give the money to the owner. Then the farmer himself must be watched by the *Mälguzär,* the *Patwäri,* the revenue inspector, or some other representative of the government, lest he sell his grain and make away with the money without paying his taxes. These minor officers of the government must be under surveillance lest they conspire with the farmer to cheat the government. So a great amount of machinery is required and an elaborate system of checks and counterchecks to enable the government to collect its revenue. Revenue is derived principally from land tax, salt tax, excise, income tax, licenses and octroi.

In the police department similar difficulties are found. Bribery is very common. If a crime is committed and the native police is given good "hush money," it is very difficult for the English officers to

bring the guilty party to light. On the other hand, it not infrequently happens that the police try to make business more lively by trumping up a case against an innocent party, with the hope of securing either a present from the accused as the price of abandoning the case or receiving favor from the superior officer for sagacity in the detection of crime.

Like perplexities embarrass the judicial department. A lawyer can get any number of witnesses to swear to anything he may dictate by paying two to four *annas* (4 to 8 cents) to each witness for his services. Of course, perjury is severely punished when it is clearly proven, but the art of dissembling is so highly developed and the schemes are so minutely elaborated that a very shrewd judge is required to detect a witness in a lie.

One case will illustrate a large class of the false-swearing: In a certain village a *Patel* (head man of the village) became too familiar with the reputed wife of the village watchman. The watchman went to the Patel's house and gave him a severe beating, using as his weapon his shoe, which is supposed to disgrace the recipient of the chastisement to the last degree. It is very rare that a humble man will dare to strike so important personage as a Patel; but in this case the watchman was furious that his home had been defiled, though he himself had never been lawfully married to the woman in question. After returning to his house the watchman bethought himself that the Patel had not yet received sufficient punishment for his misdeed and should be brought into court. But if he were

Railways, telegraphs, electric power, factories, commerce, methodical and systematic government, schools and colleges have been mighty forces for the uplifting and development of the country. But all these have come through European civilization. The more thoughtful of the native population recognize these benefits and are grateful for them. The people generally are content with the present rule. There are some agitators there, as in all countries, who endeavor to excite opposition, but with little success. India has large possibilities for development and the British have the opportunity and the power to accomplish great things in that important part of the Orient.

CHAPTER III.

MISSIONS IN INDIA.

There are many missionary societies at work in India; yet hundreds, even thousands of towns and villages have never been visited by a missionary. According to the Missionary Directory there are ten Baptist societies with 256 missionaries; two Congregational societies with 159 missionaries; ten Church of England societies with 515 missionaries; fifteen Presbyterian societies with 460 missionaries; three Methodist societies with 298 missionaries; ten Lutheran societies with 259 missionaries; two Moravian societies with 27 missionaries; two Friends' or Quaker Societies with 25 missionaries; four female societies with 108 missionaries; twenty-three independent missions with 317 missionaries, making a total of eighty-two societies and 2,424 missionaries.

This would give the missionaries about 123,000 souls each to care for, if they could be evenly distributed among the 300,000,000 of India's people. To build up a successful mission in a center, schools, (day and boarding), workshops, colleges here and there, zenana work, training-classes and many other departments of work, are indispensable. The stations now occupied as mission centers are about 640.

Most of the people reached belong to the low-caste, and are very poor, ignorant, helpless, and need much teaching and care to make them intelligent and sincere Christians. The *per cent* reached among the high is almost as great. A gentleman from America, visiting in India, said he thought a converted coolie or sweeper should be just as good a Christian as a converted student or college president. Would he apply this remark in the homeland and say that a converted denizen of the slums or a converted waif should be at once as good a Christian as a converted young man from college, who not only accepts the salvation of Christ and his precepts sincerely, but does so intelligently also? Paul did not seem to find his converts quite correct in practice for some years, even though he did not charge them with insincerity. Read his epistle carefully and note the things about which he charges those babes in Christ. How carefully the Christian father and mother watch and guard the little ones in their home! They know the little hearts love God, but of how many pitfalls they must be warned! Then how much more these babes in righteousness! A missionary once said to me: "In helpfulness and wisdom they are nearly all children, but in knowledge of sin every child is a man."

The Apostle said to his people: "Little children, keep yourselves from idols." He knew how insidious idolatry is, how it creeps into the marriage and burial customs, feasts, and daily life, and how powerful is the hold of old habits and superstitions. I will quote

A GROUP OF CHRISTIANS.

the answer given by my husband in one of the home
papers to the question: "What sort of Christians have
you?"

WHAT SORT OF CHRISTIANS HAVE YOU?

The question is often asked: "What sort of
Christians have you in India?" The tone of the
questioner implies a little doubt about the saintliness
of our Christians here. We may answer that we have
various sorts of people under the Christian name.
They are not all holy. Some of them walk crooked.
Some years ago one of my native preachers, who
could speak some English, was telling me about
another brother whose character was somewhat ques-
tionable. He said: "Sahib, I feel very doubtless
about Ganpat." So there are some Christians about
whom we feel "doubtless," and shall probably feel
so until we see them inside of glory.

Sinful things happen in America, where the light
of the gospel illuminated the grandfathers and great-
grandfathers, where the shadow of the Cross falls on
every cradle and the songs of Zion are the lullabies
of every home. Here we are in a heathen land.
Lying is almost universal. A lawyer can get all the
witnesses he wants to swear to anything he
dictates for five cents a head. A groceryman who
would give full weight every time without being
watched would be looked upon with suspicion. Little
girls of many of the higher castes are put behind the
purdah and are kept practically locked up to keep
them pure. Boys of thirteen or fourteen and girls
of ten or twelve become husband and wife that they
may not violate the rules of decency. A Hindu
told me recently that in a certain town of 10,000 people probably not one in twelve was chaste. I think
the condition is better, however, than he estimated.

In an atmosphere like this, where from childhood up—yes, from past generations—sin of every
kind has abounded, and has been looked upon as so
light a thing, is it any wonder that some of our
converts find it difficult to comprehend at once and

live up to the Christian standard? After Paul had
preached a long time in Corinth and indoctrinated
the people in the truths of the Gospel he went to
another city; but after some time he heard that one
of the young church members at Corinth was living
with his father's wife, and that the church thought
so little of it that they had not even disciplined the
young man. I never heard of a case like that in
India.

We occasionally have someone here, like Paul's
Hymenæus and Alexander, who has to be turned over
to the devil. But, on the other hand, we have others
like Pandita Ramabai, who, although coming out of
the moral slime of India, are spotless white lilies
with hearts of gold. The Church in India is taking
hold of Christ and his truth, and, considering the
hole of the pit, from which it has been digged, the
moral degradation of the heathen from among whom
our Christians have come, the washing of regeneration and renewing of the Holy Ghost are very marked
in the Indian Church.

This is an answer, brief and to the point; but many
wonderful examples of deeply spiritual lives might be
cited in our Hindustan Church, comprising all denominations. A little item which I noticed once in
some notes of a correspondent from Rangoon might
be given to show that even among the unlettered converts there is often deep conscientiousness about their
Christian duty. Near Toungoo there is a large number of Christian Karens, whom the Baptist missionaries have taught to especially honor the Sabbath day.
An English district official, while on tour, decided to
strike camp and make a march one Sunday. To this
end he made requisition for transport upon a neighboring Karen village. Imagine his surprise when the
Karen headman told him that, as it was Sunday, he

and his people must spend the day as they believed right; but on the next day would be ready to help him on his journey. The official's dignity was offended and he laid hands on the Karen and maltreated him. A missionary sought redress from the official, but, obtaining none, appealed to higher officials. The official Sabbath-breaker was severely reprimanded, and the Lieutenant Governor said, in his reply: "I am authorized to say that his honor would discountenance any attempt to compel Christian natives of the country to work on Sunday."

Many suffer persecution of the most violent kind, and yet remain true to their profession of faith in Christ. Others, while not tormented bodily, go through extreme mental suffering on account of losing friends, family—all, when they come out openly as Christians. This was the case of Sooboo Nagam Ammal, whose story appears in this chapter. We know a young Parsee lad in Poona who was converted in Bombay at the street-preaching of the missionaries and their helpers. His family cast him off entirely and he found employment in an office at thirty rupees (ten dollars) per month. This, to him, was starvation pay, as he had been used to every luxury. Too poor to even ride on the street cars, he would stand on a corner and watch the elegant equipage of his father roll by, containing his proud mother and beautiful sisters in rich silks and costly jewels. This young man finally entered a training-class in Poona to fit himself for a Gospel worker, never expecting to re-

ceive any more worldly aid than the pittance paid him
in the office.

Another young man, a former Brahmin, was so
humble and devout that he willingly taught a school
composed of sweeper-boys. Earnest Christians at home
are not always willing to teach once a week in a negro
school, yet this could not evidence their devotion as
did the act of the Brahmin youth, for whatever our
race prejudices, in our religion we are taught that
there is neither Jew nor Greek, bond nor free; while
this boy's teaching from childhood had been to regard
the Sudra and the out-caste as unworthy even to be
touched or to hear the truth.

Another young man we know about was tied to a
beam in the room, an ax held over him and threatened
with having his tongue burned through for uttering
the name of Jesus.   His father-in-law, for he had
been married in childhood, had his little girl's head
shaved in token that she was a widow; yet none of
these things moved this brave young spirit.

In the Khassia Hills, in the Welsh mission near
Shillong, there is a Christian village.   The few who
have not yet become real Christians, join the others in
observing the Sabbath.   An old chief, or sirdar there,
for years used to bring an annual thank-offering to the
Lord of a tenth of all his earnings, besides giving a
monthly subscription to the ministry and other objects.
On one occasion he asked a missionary to write down
each item of income received during the year.   Then
he said: "Add them up and divide by ten, that I may
know how much I owe to the Lord."   That evening, at

a church-meeting, the old chief brought a large bundle of rupees and laid it on the table as his thank-offering to his Lord and Master.

If many county chiefs in Christian lands would bring similar bundles to the Lord yearly, how fast the Gospel-car would move! Many steadfast and deeply spiritual Christians are well known to all who have worked in India. Zahur Ul-Haqq of North India, who became a presiding elder in the American Methodist mission, was a grand man, who after much persecution had the happiness of winning both wife and sons to the Christian religion. In the American mission at Nagar a Hindu boy attending the school was converted, who but recently, after a long and devoted life, went to his reward. This was Ramchandra Babaji Powar. When he decided to openly confess his faith he was subjected to great persecution. When his mother found that he was firm she beat her breast with a large stone until it swelled. Then she went home and hid herself in a dark chamber and was never seen by anyone until the day she died, a few months after. This news almost overwhelmed Mr. Powar, but he was sustained by his trust in God. He was baptized by the Rev. Murray Mitchell and received into the Free Church. He taught his little girl-wife the truths of the Christian religion and she, too, was at length baptized. He was well-educated and received offers of government service, but refused all to preach God's word; yet he would not be ordained, as he thought it wrong to call a man reverend."

You might extend this list and have a modern eleventh chapter of Hebrews, for time would fail to tell of the faith of Ramabai, Chundra Leela, the converted fakir, and of many others in the Indian Christian Church.

What more wonderful story of heroism than that of Sooboo Nagam Ammal? She belonged to a proud, high-caste family in Madras. Her father was a judge in the High Court and her husband was in government employ. She was a pet and indulged favorite at home, for her husband had never taken her to his home, as she was one of a pair of twins and born on a Friday; so her coming would bring misfortune to his house. She was honored as a married woman, however, and riches and position count in India as elsewhere. To her was intrusted the worship of the gods, and in all ceremonies and rites she became proficient. Her desire to become perfect in all these caused her to long for the accomplishment of reading, as then she could read the sacred Vedas and know more about the will of the gods. At this time she was having manufactured a golden image of herself bowing before her favorite god. This was to adorn a temple which she was building with her own means. No one could be found who would teach her except the Zenana Mission workers. This greatly disturbed her people.

"Yes, they will teach you to read, but they will also teach you this new religion about Jesus."

"No, no," Sooboo told them. "What they teach me about *that* will go in one ear and out the other."

The lessons of this newer and purer religion did not go out, however, but sank into an earnest and inquiring heart, for the haughty Brahmin bowed at the feet of the lowly man of Nazareth and learned of him. Her hope was that she might remain in her home and teach her relatives and friends. But this, in an orthodox Hindu house, is well-nigh impossible. Persuasions, caresses, then coldness, and finally persecution followed. A plot was set on foot by which they hoped to spirit her away to a temple in Bangalore and there dedicate her to the god of the temple. In connection with thousands of temples in India there are houses for the poor girls who are married to the gods. These, in reality, become the temple prostitutes. In Western India, around Poona, hundreds of little girls are married in this way to "Khandoba." Even a beautiful Eurasian child was with difficulty saved from this fate, which her heathen mother had planned. When Sooboo heard this she fled at night to the missionaries' bungalow. Here her friends and relatives followed to persuade her to return; but she had chosen the true God, and Jesus, whom He had sent to redeem men.

When persuasion and threats all failed her family made an effigy of Sooboo, which they carried through the streets, wailing out: "Sooboo is dead! Sooboo is dead!" As she listened to this she found it almost unbearable. But finally she took her fingers from her ears, realizing that Sooboo, the once proud, "twice-born" *Brahmin* Sooboo, was *indeed* dead; but that she was alive again in Christ, who can do all things. The effigy was burned on the funeral-pyre and Sooboo's

well. This aroused a great storm. The Hindus appealed to the courts to protect their wells from the despised Christians. Vishnupunt Karmarkar was summoned and urged not to disturb the peace-loving Hindus. He, however, stood firmly for his rights, requesting the judge to deal with the case according to the law, which gave him liberty to use the public wells. The judge referred the matter to the Bombay government. From there it went to the Viceroy and then to the Queen, who decided in favor of the native Christians. (Res. No. 34, 9th August, 1860.)

Vishnu Karmarkar founded a printing-press in Bombay, which his sons operated for some years after his death. His elder brother was converted at one of his services of song. Having given up caste, position and family, he has founded a new family of Christian Karmarkars, who are prominent in Christian benevolence and usefulness. Both sons are in the ministry, one being a Yale divinity graduate, while the daughter gives her time and energy to teaching a class of poor children in Colaba, Bombay.

As this old veteran was dying he asked his children to sing :—

> Oh! happy day that fixed my choice
> On thee my Saviour and my God.

Then he said: "Open the door and let me fly above. I desire to enter a large place."

CHUNDRA LEELA.

This woman, when left a widow, determined to spend her life in securing peace of soul. In order to do this she went to shrine after shrine, visiting Jaga-

A BIBLE CART IN INDIA.

(*From an electro supplied by the Zenana Bible and Medical Mission.*)

nath, Benares, Ramanath and many other sacred sites.
At one time she sat among the "seven fires." That is,
fires built all around her and the blazing May sun over
head. Seeking truth she went about begging bread
and inflicting torture upon herself until she heard the
Gospel story—and her fetters were broken. Ever
since then she has gone about, seemingly tireless,
teaching her new faith and the redemptive power of
Christ, and anxious to do as much for her loving
Savior as she used to do for heathen gods. These
are some of the trophies of Christian missions. But
we may not speak of these only. The failure and
apostasy of the weak ones should spur us on to teach
and preach more indefatigably. What may we expect
in a land of heathen darkness and among a people used
to idolatry and its practices?

Sometimes village Christians, untutored and superstitious, are drawn away by the sophistry of the old
priests whom they feared and obeyed before they em-
braced Christianity. One of the saddest as well as
one of the most tragic of such events was told me by
a person most intimately concerned and affected.
Phœbe Rowe was among our most remarkable and
most devoted of Eurasian evangelists. She gave her
life to labor among the low-caste Christians. Especially
did her heart go out to the women in such commu-
nities. One day she went, in company with Mother
Catherine and the native pastor, to visit a village which
could receive but scant pastoral care on account of the
amount of work put upon one pair of shoulders. When
they entered the town everything was in the greatest

confusion. All the inmates of the little mud-huts had congregated in an open space, where, led by the priests of their caste, they had set up a shrine to "Lall Beg," the red prince, and were preparing to offer cocks as sacrifice to him. The poor, weak Christians were abashed at the appearance of their pastor and the beloved evangelist and her helper. After much pleading by the latter, and noisy threatenings from the priests, who saw that their craft was in danger, the people declared their willingness to return to allegiance to the Christians' God.

"Then destroy the shrine," the pastor suggested. But, looking at the angry priests, they were afraid to comply. In spite of their better judgment, they feared disaster would follow such a daring act.

"May I do it?" the pastor asked, for he feared its presence among them. They consented and the poor little shrine of clay and lime was soon utterly demolished. The pastor, however, wishing to demonstrate the nothingness of the idol, called on him (Lall Beg) to destroy him if he had any power.

"Let Lall Beg destroy me to-night if he has any power," he said.

At about eleven o'clock Miss Rowe was called to the pastor's tent, to find him in violent convulsions, and in a few hours he was dead. Miss Rowe herself felt weak and ill, and soon after went to the hills, where she, too, died after two weeks. Shall we attribute this to the machinations of the baffled priests, or is it possible that it was a coincidence? We do not believe it could have been a mere coincidence. Miss

HARDWICKE CHRISTIAN BOYS' SCHOOL, NARSINGHPUR.
This building was once the palace of a petty Rajah.

Rowe, in writing to me about it, said that it was the most depressing thing that had ever come into her experience. Of course, many in that village and many in surrounding villages returned to "Lall Beg's" worship. Can we hope to find no apostasy amid such hoary heathenism as that of India?

But it is not only among the high-caste that we find such conversions as Karmarkar's, Powar's, Pundita Ramabai's, or Kali Bannerjee's, a pleader in the High Court of Calcutta, but many among the humble people, are faithful even unto death.

Many low-caste boys and girls are attaining to honorable positions in the community and are winning thousands of their own people. Amid persecution which has never touched us; amid heathen superstitions and iron-bound caste-rules, is growing up a people from many peoples; a noble brotherhood and sisterhood having one faith, one ambition, one hope, one God.

ORPHANAGES IN INDIA.

In all the various missions in India, supported by money from America, Great Britain, Australia and other countries, we find these beneficent institutions. Thousands of homeless children are gathered into these orphanages, cared for, instructed and trained for useful lives.

During years of famine in India, when the harvests fail, is the time for the great harvest of children to be gathered into these orphanages and trained and taught in the pure religion of Christ. Many orphanages were born of the famine of 1876-77 and, during the famine

study is that prescribed by the government in the various vernaculars of India.   Most of the schools receive grants appropriated to tuition from government funds, depending upon the examinations.   This is really a very small amount.   The bulk of the support is from benevolent people in Christian lands, for food and clothing and shelter must be provided as well as instruction.   The opportunity for religious and moral training is very important.   Adult converts rid themselves of heathen practices and superstitions but slowly, especially if uneducated and ignorant, but the children in these schools, in very many instances, attain a Christian character which, without such training, is seldom reached until the second or third generation of Christianizing.

A missionary of over forty years' experience in India, who has herself been for years in charge of a large orphanage, gives the following recommendation to the boys and girls she has known to go out from the schools.   She says: "Some of our best teachers and preachers were educated in our orphanages; some fill important positions; some are good doctors and, indeed, I don't know how we could have gone on with our work without the help we have had from the orphan boys and girls."

These children, who are not cared for by their families, become our very own, and, while undoubtedly some prove unthankful and return to Hinduism and Mohammedanism, yet the great majority become instructors of their own people, build up the Christian church in India and exemplify Christian living in a dark and idolatrous land.

CLASS OF BOYS STUDYING ENGLISH IN HARDWICKE CHRISTIAN BOYS' SCHOOL.

CHAPTER IV.

CITY OF THE PESHWAS.

Poona, called the City of the Peshwas, was at one time the scene of Sivaji's warlike glory, and afterward that of the Peshwas, who had their rise under Sivaji's grandson. This grandson was, for a long time, held in captivity by the Mohammedans, among whom he learned habits of luxury and indolence and became very unlike his warlike ancestors. When he came into possession of his kingdom he resigned the management of his territories to his prime minister, giving him the title of Peshwa. This title and authority became hereditary, and the power of the Peshwas soon exceeded that of the kings. These Peshwas built up the great Maratha Confederacy, having its headquarters in Poona. While the Marathas have no distinct political power, yet here they still hold bigoted and almost undisputed religious sway; here, too, is the seat of much political unrest and occasional outbreaks against the English government.

It would be difficult to find a finer race of men than the Maratha Brahmins, and their dress is calculated to accentuate their naturally attractive appearance. Their *pugries* or head-dresses are very becoming, and the gold threads woven into the cloth from which the *pugries* are made, give an effect of richness and refinement to their heads. The women are not

kept in *purdah* as are most high-class Hindu and Mohammedan women in other parts of India. While the
male and female members of the household live very
separate lives, and there is nothing to correspond to
our ideas of society and social equality of the sexes,
yet the women are seen driving about the city and
in the parks and going on foot as well, without covering their faces unless to ward off a particularly imper-
tinent stare. The Marathi women (the ending *a* is
masculine while the *i* is feminine) would be much finer
looking were it not for their manner of dressing their
hair, which is drawn back so tightly that it causes total
or partial baldness on the sides and crown of the head.
They wear many jewels and a company of the younger
women, who still have plenty of black hair, when in
holiday attire, present a very attractive appearance.

The city of Poona has now a population of 130,000.
It is built on a bare, rocky plateau of the western ghäts,
about 2,000 feet above the sea. It is surrounded by
rocks and hills and the level stretches are very barren
in appearance. In and about the city, particularly
in the Cantonments, or European section, there are
beautiful tree-lined drives and avenues.

The city is considered healthy for the most part,
but during the time of plague it had an awful visita-
tion. The sanitary measures considered necessary by
government, were strongly resented by the people,
especially the inspection of houses, which was looked
upon as an interference with sacred customs and an
insult to the privacy of the women. Many wives of
English officials, appreciating both the prejudices of

AMERICAN MISSIONARY IN MARATHI COSTUME.

GROUP OF HIGH-CASTE YOUTHS, POONA, INDIA.

this proud people and also the necessity on the part of government to stay the plague by all possible, lawful means, stepped nobly into the breach and volunteered to visit the houses themselves in place of the soldiers deputed for this work. Even this sacrifice did not prevent much disturbance, which culminated in the murder of two English officials.

The population is of high-and-low-caste Hindus, a good portion of Mohammedans and 8,000 Europeans, including the English soldiers. In the native city there is an institution for the education of high-caste youths, and Poona claims to have had the first girls' school in India. In the English portion there are comfortable bungalows, as the better sort of houses are called, and many schools and colleges. On the occasion of a great fête, given by the Governor's wife to all European school-children, there were present 1,400 children. This suggests the importance of the European element in the city. The crowded native city, with its bazaars of cloth-shops and sweetmeat stands, and with brass and other wares, is very interesting. Some of the unique curios in Poona are the *putlies,* or images done in clay and colored most artistically and true to life. These represent the various castes and occupations in Indian society and life.

All classes sit on the floor while eating and use brass or silver plates. If the company is large, green leaves, such as the banana leaf, may do duty as plates. All eat with their fingers. Much of the cooking is very palatable and pleasant.

At a wedding breakfast we saw a curious custom.

ing in all this flummery; but as he had succeeded to
this position on the death of his brother, his family
would be disgraced if he refused.   It was a lucrative
place.   Why should he not take it?   It was probably
this same priest who gave the striking and perchance
prophetic answer to Bishop Foster, who, in company
with Bishop Thoburn, visited this temple.   The bishop
asked him: "How long has all this worship been
going on here?"   "For thousands of years" was the
reply.   "And how long will it last?" the bishop inquired.   "Not long," the young priest replied.   "And
why," continued the bishop.   The Hindu hesitated, but
raising his hand and pointing with his finger he swept
the line of the horizon and simply said, "Jesus."   It
was the old prophecy in the grand old hymn:

> Jesus shall reign where'er the sun
> Does his successive journeys run;
> His kingdom spread from shore to shore
> Till moons shall wax and wane no more.

These idols are bathed, fed, put to sleep and
awakened.   The idea is that the image imprisons a
spirit which is pleased with libations of oil or butter
and offerings of grain and flowers.   The spirit con-
sumes the ethereal portion of the food while the priests
take the substantial, as is well evidenced by their fat
and flourishing condition.

When putting the idol to sleep, unearthly music
on conch shells and other queer instruments is made.
A similar noise, with the addition of some bell-ringing
serves to awaken him.   No wonder the prophet of old
told the people derisively to cry aloud, as perchance
their god slept or had gone on a journey.   Judging

from the almost incessant noise in some temples, the god must be a sort of Morpheus. Washings, prayers, offerings and caste-observances—these are the religion of the Hindu, with the Brahmin as his spiritual head, if the term spiritual may be applied to cruelty, avarice and moral decay. Religion is not connected with morality, as we understand it. To eat with a low-caste man is a far more heinous crime than to lie, steal or commit adultery, if these things are done in a way that shall not hurt caste. In each caste there is a *Panchaiyat* or council of five and this council regulates or decides upon the permissibility of certain acts or of conduct in general, while the outward worship is offered to the gods. Thus they follow cunningly devised fables and degrade the God-head to the level of the loathsome creatures represented by the idols. This is the essence of idolatry. It is not a harmless bowing down to wood and stone, as many in Western lands imagine it. There is an inwardness, corresponding to this outward worship, which is full of vileness and corruption. Many otherwise inexplicable traits in the people become plain as we search for the meaning of these rites and symbols of idolatry. The gods and goddesses worshiped in the guise of wood and stone and gold, are impure and full of uncleanness. No wonder, even in beautiful Athens, before the Acropolis crowned with its marvelous temples of the gods, that Saint Paul's heart was filled with grief as he saw the people wholly given over to idolatry. How much more in India, where there is not even esthetic beauty to gloss over the moral corruption of the gods! For as

the gods are, so shall the people become. But all this shall indeed not last long, as the Brahmin said. Some day on Parwati another temple shall stand, containing no idol or shrine and only witnessing the offerings of meek and lowly hearts, and the worship shall be that of Jesus.

CHAPTER V.

CHILD-WIDOWS.

The stories of one little widow, and of Runabai, given in later chapters, exhibit the condition of child-widows in a sufficiently strong light, yet, lest some may think these are isolated cases, a few additional facts and examples may be valuable to show that their lot is always a pitiable one, though they are not treated with equal severity in all parts of India.

Among the various nationalities in India, Hindus form the larger proportion. Altogether there are 140,000,000 women in India, while among the Hindus alone there are 23,000,000 widows. Taking from these the aged widows, widows with families and widows of all but the two higher castes, Sir William Hunter says that "there can be no less than one million young widows of the Brahmin and Rajput castes to whom the system of enforced celibacy must be held to be a cruel infringement of their natural rights." These were widowed in early childhood. He further says that, adding these to young women in other high castes, there can be no less than two million of widows to whom the existing Hindu law is an injustice and a wrong. These two million women are equal in number to all the women in Scotland. All Hindu girls at the age of fifteen are either wives or widows. This is, of course, owing to the system of child-marriage

which was instituted to escape the disgrace of having
an unmarried daughter on the parents' hands. In 1856
a law was passed by the English government legalizing
the remarriage of widows.   Some few earnest reformers have been brave enough to marry educated
widows from Pandita Ramabai's school, and, here and
there, similar cases occur; but the iron law of custom
is so strong that few are able to face the terrible
ostracism and boycotting resulting from such a pro-
cedure.   The widow, if she marries, loses all claim
to her first husband's property, though if she remains
unmarried and lives a sinful life she can still hold her
inheritance.

Rammohun Roy, India's greatest modern reformer,
accomplished much against fearful odds for the elevation of women.   He was the first native of rank and
influence who broke through the invincible prejudice
of centuries and crossed the "black water."   He arrived in England in 1830 and did all he could to prevent the repeal of the bill abolishing *sati* (usually
written as pronounced, *suttee*).   This bill was passed
in 1829, through his exertions, and has never been
repealed.   For years before the horrible custom of
immolating widows on the funeral pyre of their husbands had been forbidden by law, the English officials
used to be present to give the widow a fair chance of
escape, if at last she repented of the assent she had
given to the fearful rite.   Previous to the English rule
the priests were accustomed to force her back upon the
pyre to fulfill her vow.   Although this dreadful custom has been abolished for nearly three-quarters of a

century, yet so sad is the lot of the widow that, as a Hindu expresses it, "she now endures *cold suttee.*"

Mrs. Fuller quotes a number of Indian gentlemen in regard to the woes of Indian women and the disadvantage under which they labor, and I shall take a few of these quotations because some may think that missionaries, seeing isolated cases, magnify the condition as a whole. Some men and women of India, being happily situated themselves, deny the statements because they have not come into personal contact with suffering. Hence they find it difficult to believe it exists.

In our own land and in England, how many favored women know absolutely nothing of the sorrows of the slums in their own cities! Pundita Ramabai has said that when she was sixteen or seventeen years of age, although she had visited nearly every sacred shrine in India with her parents and brother, yet she was so shielded that she never knew of the evils then, which in later life she so graphically set forth after seeing them herself. Many live very exclusive lives in their own caste and know very little of what occurs in other castes about them. We take a quotation from the "Indian Social Reform" of December, 1898:

> In the days of my early childhood, in those days when the mind can hardly penetrate through the thick folds of mystery which shroud half the things of this world, my simple mind was drawn to the subject of the Hindu Widow. Her melancholy attire, her disfigured head, her care-worn appearance, the rude way in which she is handled by our society, all these created in me the impression that the widow somehow belonged not to the ranks of the two recog-

peated bathings so as not to go hungry. During Dr. Pentecost's meeting he was induced to come and hear the Gospel. The day after he attended the meeting he was taken ill. When we called there he had high fever. We talked a little to him. He said:

"Wasn't it strange that after I had heard one sermon I should be laid by like this? But God will do right. I am trusting myself to him."

He never rose from that fever. He wanted to write out his will regarding his wife—how she should be treated—as he abhorred the custom of ill-treating widows. Of course, he could not leave her any property or place her in an independent position, as all the property was held jointly by the brothers; still it is probable that had he written his desire to have her placed in Ramabai's care to be educated, his brothers might have respected his wish. But pen and paper were refused him and no one would write for him. When Ramabai heard of his death, she said:

"Poor Mrs. Kirteney! His parents are orthodox Hindus; the property was joint; she is at the mercy of the household."

It is hard to realize the utter helplessness of the Hindu widow. Many stories could be written by those who go about in high-caste homes and see the poor shaven heads and the little figures hiding in corners or behind doors. I always single them out for kind words and notice, but they are almost too timid to respond. They think it a favor if someone is kind enough to motion them to leave their drudgery and listen to the hymns we sing and which the women love

so much to hear. Before I knew much about the widow's lot I used ignorantly to ask in regard to one of these crouching, timid figures: "Who is that?" No one ever told me her name or relationship. Simply pointing the thumb over the shoulder (she was sure to be in the background) and giving a contemptuous jerk of the chin, the answer was: "Only a widow."

One dear little girl in Ramabai's school received word that as she was now twelve years old, it was time for her to break off her little armlets and have her head shaved. She must come home for these degrading things to be done and the father thought they wuold keep her at home to wash and cook and scrub. The child was nearly frantic. Every time she heard wheels she would run and hide. She begged not to be sent back, but Ramabai was powerless. But the father never came for the child. In Ramabai's words: "He meant to come and take her back to misery, but he died." The child was overjoyed at the news.

Do not read all this about the baby and girl-widows and think of it as a far-away story of a far-away, unreal land, but picture your own golden or brown-haired darling as one of these widows in India. Little children, two million of them, crying to be delivered from the curse implied in that word, *"widow!"*

PUNDITA RAMABAI, THE WIDOWS' CHAMPION.

When we came to India, ten years ago, one of the pleasures to which I looked forward was meeting the little Christian woman, once a Brahmin widow, who had done so much for her afflicted Indian sisters, suf-

intervals, and I wondered what the sight could mean. The next day I learned from an inmate of the home that Rai had remained up there in the stillness all night to pray for a troublesome girl. The strong faith and devotion of this Indian sister is a rebuke to many who have known the religion of Christ from infancy. She showed me a small idol, which, at the age of twenty-one, she was in the habit of worshiping. She was thoroughly versed in the sacred books or Vedas. Yet in less than twenty-one years she had attained to such a marvelous Christian experience and been made so useful in working for others!

Her acceptance of the Christian religion, or rather of Christ himself, was a gradual one. A personal letter, quoted some years ago in a paper published in India, shows very clearly the steps by which she has been led along from a philosophic belief in the Bible, as containing the best religion, to a vital faith in Jesus Christ. These are her words:

> I simply believed that God would save me if I repented of my sins; that it was to declare his readiness to forgive all sins of those who repented that God sent Christ into this world. So here I was, a professed Christian, but not converted, as I understand the word now. I had repented and was continually asking God to forgive my sins; but the great burden remained on my heart, just as it had been there before I was baptized. I gave up reading theological books and betook myself to the Bible. I was still going on with my old belief, when some time ago it pleased God to draw me nearer to him by bringing a great affliction on me. In this I recognized the hand of the loving Father and began more and more to cast all my cares upon him, instead of trusting in my own strength and human friends;

but the difficulties were staring me in the face just as they did the lawyer in the tenth chapter of Luke. One very hot night, made hotter by the struggle that was going on within me, I opened the Bible and found this promise: "For a small moment have I forsaken thee; but with great mercies will I gather thee." My soul began to realize its utter helplessness and misery, the many failures of best intentions and resolutions. I fully understood that I could not help myself, so I set aside all my doubts and resolved to take the Lord at his word. I surrendered to him, trusting that he would do what was right by me. Since then a great burden is taken away from my heart and almost all my doubts have gone. The old Vedantic philosophy had so much occupied my mind that there was little room for anything else. According to it, God is a being who has neither sorrow nor joy. The pure essence of God cannot suffer, cannot feel for man. I had already believed John iii:16, but my difficulty was not removed. One night, as I was returning home, it suddenly dawned on me that our God is a God of love. God is love itself. He is not the passive being of the Vedanta who cannot feel for man. It is therefore most natural for God to sympathize with man and come to his help in his sore need. I feel very happy over this, and thank God with all my heart that he sent Jesus Christ to save me by taking my sins away.

This letter, however, while clear and beautiful, does not fully portray the deep reality of Ramabai's spiritual life—the childlike faith and the robust, yet simple working out of her belief amid the perplexities of her position.

One of her most noticeable traits is her indifference to public notice and applause. She goes on quietly with her work of rescue and love, seldom attending large assemblies or public gatherings, unless by so do-

ing she can forward the work she loves. At the De-
cennial Conference of Missionaries, held in Bombay in
1892, Ramabai was announced to address a large meeting. Hundreds of missionaries of all denominations
were anxious to see and hear this apostle of female
education and reform; but Ramabai did not come.
One of her beloved "girls" was taken very ill, and, like
a tender mother, she remained by the bedside. Many
very devoted missionaries would have left the child in
the care of a trustworthy assistant and been present
themselves at the meeting to give and receive help and
inspiration. One of her children was ill; she could not
leave. There was no thought of applause nor honor;
only, the anxiety of a mother.

Her work has now grown to marvelous propor-
tions. The school for widows in Poona continues;
but, when the famine of 1896-97 desolated India,
Ramabai stretched forth her hands to save three hundred women and girls. This she accomplished. She
herself had known famine and had subsisted for days
upon leaves of trees; so her whole heart went out to
rescue and to save. The means were always forth-
coming and a settlement was started at Khedgaon, a
small village outside of Poona. Here farming was
carried on and the girls and women were taught and
employed. Then came the famine of 1900, and the
numbers at Mukti, as the settlement is called, increased, until now Ramabai's family of girls and
widows numbers nineteen hundred. Missionaries
help her in holding services, and she has a noble band
of workers; but her own hand is on everything and

GROUP OF CHILD WIDOWS

PORTRAIT OF RAMABAI

her presence felt everywhere. Out of this great company of homeless famine waifs will come teachers, wives of Christian men, and Christian nurses and servants.

Not less wonderful than her work is her own history, and, of course, the two are inseparably united. But for her early training she would have had no knowledge of Sanscrit; without it, she could not have obtained the position as lecturer and instructor in the Calcutta College, and afterwards in England as professor of Sanscrit in Cheltenham College, Oxford. To comprehend how Ramabai has obtained the scholarship which is hers, it is necessary to know something of the aspiration and thoughts of one of the advanced thinkers of India, for such undoubtedly was Ramabai's father. This man, Ananta Shastri, a Brahmin pundit, had in his student days met a very talented princess. His astonishment on hearing a woman recite Sanscrit poems made him resolve that his little child-wife should also become learned. To this her parents were opposed and he was never able to have his wish. After her death he met Ramabai's mother, then a little girl of nine. She and her parents and sister were on a religious pilgrimage, when they stopped at a certain town for a few days' rest. One day the little girl's father was bathing in the sacred Godaveri, when he saw a fine-looking man approaching. After the ablutions and prayers were finished the father asked the stranger his name and from whence he came. On learning his caste, clan and condition, he offered him his nine-year-old girl as a wife. The pundit saw the opportunity of

fulfilling his dream of having an educated wife and
very gladly accepted the child. The next day the marriage was concluded and the father departed with a
light heart, knowing nothing of his son-in-law, yet
feeling that he had done the best possible for his young
daughter in getting her properly married. She was
tenderly cared for, but when her husband undertook
her education, his mother raised a perfect storm of
threats and pleadings. He was not to be baffled in his
second attempt, so he took his girl-wife up into the
Western Ghats, on a remote plateau, and there, literally
in the jungle, he conducted the education of the little
girl who afterwards became Ramabai's mother. She
became proficient in the Vedas and in the knowledge
of Sanscrit. Ramabai treasures still a manuscript book
from which her mother taught her. When Ramabai
was born, in 1858, her father was growing quite old
and almost unable to teach the students who flocked to
him. Ramabai's mother taught her almost entirely.
When Ramabai was nine years old the family set out
on a religious pilgrimage, as is the custom among
many high-caste families. It was decided as a special
favor to delay Ramabai's marriage until she was sixteen, as she was learning so rapidly.

During this pilgrimage both parents died, and the
brother and sister prepared them for burial. Often
during this time the family was almost reduced to
starvation. When the parents died the brother and
sister traveled throughout India, advocating female
education. At Calcutta her scholarship attracted the
notice of the pundits there, and she was publicly given

the title of Pundita Sarasvati. Here she was married, but after a brief, though happy wedded life, became a widow. This forcibly drew her attention to the unfortunate class of women and children in India who are perpetual widows. Her aim now was to reach England and America, in order to secure a better education in methods of teaching, and, if possible, help for her enterprise of founding a home for widows. For a time she was professor of Sanscrit in Cheltenham College, England. Here some friends came forward to help her, but her scheme was not fairly launched until she was met by the warmth of Western enthusiasm. American women received her as an equal and comrade. Soon, all over America, circles were formed called "Ramabai Circles," and an association organized which guaranteed support for ten years, by which time Ramabai hoped her own people would awake to the benefits of such an institution and would assist her in educating young widows. Many Hindus professed themselves friends of the cause, but Ramabai found that only among Christians was true charity a reality, and, since the dissolution of the association, such friends have poured into her hands the means for caring for her hundreds of dependent wards. Here, truly, is a work of faith, and she herself one of India's chosen ones.

Because of her diffidence, many do not know how much ability she possesses. Max Müller, the eminent Sanscrit scholar, cites her as having one of the most remarkable memories in the world—for a woman, the most remarkable. He invited some of his friends, pro-

fessors in the university, to meet her and test her memory, when she recited any part of the Rig Veda or Bhagavad-gita which they chose to select, and she could go on until they were tired.   She knew by heart an amount equal to the contents of our entire Bible, and, now that she is a Christian, she studies the Bible with the same avidity with which she once pored over the ancient philosophies of India.   Those old systems she finds hollow and empty, and the few beautiful things found in the books are almost nowhere carried into practice.

In speaking of her visit to Agra*, she says:

> I beg of my Western sisters not to be satisfied with looking on the outside beauty of the grand philosophies, nor to be charmed with hearing the long and interesting discourses of our educated men, but to open the trap-doors of the great monuments of ancient Hindu intellect and enter into the dark cellars where they will see the real workings of the philosophies which they admire so much.   Let our Western friends come to India and live right among us.   Let them frequently go to the hundreds of sacred places where countless pilgrims throng yearly.   Let them go around Jaganath, Puri, Benares,† Gaya, Allahabad, Muttra, Brindaban, Dwarka, Pandhrapur, Udipi, Tirpatty and such other sacred cities, the strongholds of Hinduism and seats of sacred learning, where the Mahatmas and Sadhus dwell, and where the sublime philosophies are daily taught and devoutly followed.   There are thousands of priests and men learned in sacred lore who are the spiritual rulers and guides of our people.   They neglect and oppress the widows and devour widows' houses.   I have gone to many

*See reference again in chapter on "Ancient Oudh."
†See chapter on Benares.

of the so-called sacred places, lived among the people and seen enough of those learned philosophers and possessors of superior Hindu spirituality who oppress the widows and trample the poor, ignorant, low-caste people under their heels. They have deprived the widows of their birthright to enjoy pure life and lawful happiness. They send out hundreds of emissaries to look for young widows and bring them by hundreds and thousands to the sacred cities to rob them of their money and their virtue. They entice the poor, ignorant women to leave their own homes to live in the *kshetras,* or holy places, and then, after robbing them of their belongings, tempt them to yield to their unholy desires. They shut the helpless young widows into their large *mathas,* or monasteries, sell or hire them out to wicked men so long as they can get money, and when the poor, miserable slaves are no longer pleasing to their cruel masters, they turn them out in the streets to beg their bread, to suffer the horrible consequences of sin, to carry the burden of shame, and finally to die the death worse than that of a starved street-dog. Those so-called sacred places, those veritable hells on earth, have become the graveyards of countless widows and orphans. Thousands upon thousands of young widows and innocent children are suffering untold misery and dying helpless every year throughout this land, but no philosopher or mahatma has come out boldly to champion their cause and to help them. The teachers of false philosophies and lifeless spiritualities will do no good to our people. Nothing has been done by them to protect the fatherless and judge the widows. If anything has been done by anybody at all, it has been done by those people who have come under the direct influence of Christianity.

This eloquent extract shows, not only the inner decay of Hinduism, but the acuteness of Ramabai's mind, as well as her nobility of character and her fearlessness.

TO PANDITA RAMABAI.

Did cry from Macedonia come
   And find quick answer to its needs?
And shall the ear be always dumb,
   And never foot be found to speed
To heavier sorrow, greater care,
   To India's widowhood, that mourns
And sits in ashes of despair?

Nay, God hath heard, and from the skies
   A gleam of hope! For, strong to save,
From out those widowed ranks, see rise
   A noble soul, full strong and brave
To dare hard custom, and whose heart
   Is daunted not by fear or pain.
Her faith looks up. She does her part,
   She feels she shall not plead in vain.

So over seas to unknown lands,
   To unknown hearts she takes her cause,
Her cause—to loose from heavy bands;
   To free from custom's iron laws
A sisterhood of helpless ones;
   Of those whom grief alone had nursed;
To open Life's and Learning's fount
   To those whose lives were thought accursed.

And hearts were opened everywhere;
   Were opened wide to India's need.
The thought of childhood's face of care,
   The thought of cheerless widowhood,
Found in those hearts responsive chime,
   Where love of God is linked with love
For stricken ones of every clime.

So from the gifts of many a friend
   Who gave for needs so far away,
Has grown this house which soon shall send
   Into this Empire's gloom a ray—

Nay, more!—a beam of heavenly light!
   And India's millions yet shall say:
"From out our curse, our grief, our blight,
   Has come our help, our hope, our stay."

So here, to-day, with heart and voice,
   We people of such various race
Unite as one to say: "Rejoice!
   Rejoice that in this goodly place
We see the fruits of toil and love!
   Rejoice that here in learning's path
So many feet may learn to tread!
   Rejoice to know the good begun
Shall still go on when we are dead!"

Brave Ramabai, may all things fair
   And all things pure be always thine!
Yea, they are thine; for, dwelling where
   Self and self-seeking do not come,
Seeking the good of others, balm
   Unto thine own soul shall be given;
Mother to many, thou shalt know
   While still on earth some joy of Heaven.
Poona, July 26, 1892.

CHAPTER VI.

STORIES OF LITTLE GIRLS.

Fatima's parents are Mohammedans and believe in keeping women and girls like prisoners. Fatima's mother can never go out shopping as English ladies do, never pay calls or see the birds, the sunshine or the flowers. Day after day, week after week and year after year she stays in the house or goes into the little back yard surrounded by a high brick wall. She cannot even enjoy a drive in the open air. When she goes anywhere in the ox-cart, which is very seldom, the bamboo top of the cart is covered with blankets and she can see very little as she passes along. Fatima, until lately, knew very little of her mother's sad life. She ran about the front veranda and on the streets with her brothers and had a merry time. Even in India children make mud-pies or rather *chapatties,* and play their little games. So Fatima was merry and free for a short time, something like the dear happy little ones in Christian lands. But how quickly her glad days ended! Her seventh birthday came and instead of a nice birthday party and pretty presents on that day, poor Fatima's sorrows began. On the morning of that day her strict Mohammedan father said to the poor mother: "Now, Fatima is seven years old, and she must begin to keep *purdah.*" This means that she must always stay in the back part of the house or walk

about the bare little yard with the high walls. She can never look out of the front doors or windows, never run into the front veranda or go and see the shops in the bazaar as she used to do with her brothers. A veritable prisoner! Fatima's mother cried and pleaded in vain. "Oh! she is so little yet," she said, "don't keep her in *purdah* so soon. She will almost forget how the flowers and trees look by the time she grows up. Besides, she will forget and run out."

Then the father flew into a great rage and said: "It is better never to let a woman out of the house! The Koran says that the best kind of women are those who never remember seeing any man but their own husbands and sons, and the next best those who have only seen near relatives. You would like our daughter to be totally bad and see all the men in town. She will stay in from this day and you shall watch and see that she does *not* go out."

Of course, as the mother had said, Fatima would forget the cruel order, and, seeing her brothers rush out, she would start too. Then her mother would call: "Fatima, Fatima, remember the order," and the poor child would sit down and cry as if her heart would break.

Her mother said to me, "Oh! I am so glad that my two other little girls died. Here this poor child must sit down with us women until she is twelve years old. Then she will be married and her husband will keep her shut up the rest of her life." The mother's heart ached for her, but she could do nothing to help poor little black-eyed Fatima.

Now here is Tara.　Her name means a "star," but her life is not a bright one.　She is a Brahmin child and as yet is allowed to run about and play.　But her mind is going to waste.　When we asked her father if we might teach her something, he said:

"Why teach her to read?　She must cook all her life.　Besides, Tara is engaged to be married.　She is ten years old and the order has been given for her wedding-jewels to be made.　Soon we shall take her to her mother-in-law's house and she will be trained there.　If the child knew how to read her mother-in-law would think we were making a bad woman of her. Cows don't read and women are not as good as cows."

Soon little Tara will go to Lucknow to be married. She will never see any happy school-days, never be that bright and lovely being, a fair young girl in her parents' home.　In India there is an absence of young girls with their charming ways.　Only children and married women.　These two little girls I know quite well.

Now I will tell you of a young bride that my husband saw.　She was a girl of about fourteen.　Probably she had been given in marriage long before and was now going to her husband's home.

The wedding procession looked very gay.　The horses were decked with bells, silver and gold tinsel, embroidery and bright-red and purple cloths over the saddle.　My husband stopped to look at the bridal party passing.　The groom—alas! was forty or forty-five years old and was dressed very gaily.　Behind him came the little bride on a pony.　She wore beautiful

clothes and a profusion of gold and silver jewelry. But the pretty face was bowed on the pony's neck, and, above the noise of the clashing cymbals and the various other musical instruments, rose the heartrending wail of this poor, unwilling little bride, going to the house of the stern, silent man riding in front. What happiness can be in store for such a home?

The fourth child I know as well as the first two—Gungi, a little Brahmin girl. She was married when a mere baby and at seven years old became a widow. She had never seen the middle-aged man who gave her parents a sum of rupees to seal the marriage bargain. She did not know what *widow* meant, but she soon learned to understand cruelty and semi-starvation. The husband's relatives housed and half-fed the poor baby widow. "How wicked she must have been in a former life," they would say. "Who knows? She may have been a snake. and now her sins have killed her husband." For four years she endured their wicked treatment and then she was saved by a loving Christian woman, and is now in a happy home, free from cruel blows and cruel words. When in this home for little more than a year, she composed a poem about her lot while still a widow. This little poem I have translated into English as literally as I could. Here it is:

SONG OF THE HINDU WIDOW.

Come, oh come, God, my only friend,
    My heart is heavy within me;
None to my sorrow an ear will lend,
    I am a widow! Oh, set me free!

Life's path I've trod but a little way,
  But my load is too heavy to bear;
The light of gladness has fled away,
  And wet with tears the garments I wear.

I'm a little child, yet none will save.
  When five years old betrothed to age,
To age with one foot touching the grave,
  Yet when he dies, the family rage.

The family storm and curse and swear
  The little wife has caused his death!
How shall I tell how widows fare?
  O God, I have not power nor breath.

Sold into bondage, a helpless slave!
  One hundred rupees! The paltry sum
My parents took, the old man gave,
  And I was his, what'er might come!

And oh! the sorrows when he died!
  The blows and words as hard as blows,
E'en red-hot iron their hands applied;
  The scars my injured body shows.

If we commit through youth or fear,
  The smallest fault, we plead in vain;
We know full well a storm is near
  And on our backs sticks fall like rain.

And bad words thunder in our ears.
  My feet the widow's thorny way
Had found when only seven years
  Of my short life had passed away.

When but eleven, from my head
  They shaved the soft, dark locks of hair.
They counted me as with the dead;
  The dead! I wish that I were there.

Yes, with the dead I long to be.
There, surely, I'll find rest and peace.
Come, oh my God! and set me free;
In death's cold arms give me release.

The story of four little girls—the little Mohammedan prisoner, the ignorant little betrothed Brahmin,
the weeping bride and the desolate baby widow! As
your hearts yearn for them remember there are many
Fatimas behind the *purdah;* many ignorant betrothed
children like Tara; many weeping brides and more
than twenty-two million widows in India!

RUNABAI.

Like all girls of the better classes, or higher castes
in India, little Runabai was married when but a child.
In these marriages the parents make all the arrangements, and very often the little girl or boy does not
even know what is being done. There are great ceremonies which mean that the children are promised to
each other in marriage when they are grown up. One
little girl, who was a relative of Runabai's, was married
when she was in her cradle. The costly *saris,* or wed-
ding-clothes, were hung around the sides of the cradle
where the little baby was sleeping and jewels were
placed around her tiny, unconscious face. After the
ceremonies were over these gifts were laid aside for the
little bride when she should be old enough to go to the
new home.

Runabai's marriage was similar to this. Little did
she realize as she was toddling about the beautiful
rooms of her father's bungalow that her whole life was
determined for her. The bungalow, as fine houses are

called in India, was a very nice one, and lovely plants adorned the verandas and compound. All about were signs of comfort and luxury. Her parents loved her, although they were very sorry that she was not a boy. People in India are always sorry to have little girls and often they will try to hide the fact.

One day a missionary was sitting and talking in the home of a Hindu gentleman. During the conversation the missionary asked, "How many children have you?" "Three," the gentleman replied, and he called in and showed his visitor the three fine little boys of whom he was so proud. A short time after this a pretty, bright-eyed little girl came into the room and climbed upon the knee of the gentleman. "And who is this?" asked the missionary. "My daughter," replied the Hindu in evident vexation, and he would say no more.

But our little Runabai was an affectionate child and, while in her own home, she did not realize that she was not welcome. A few years of happiness were soon over; for when she was only eleven years of age the parents of her boy-husband, whom she had never seen and of whom she knew nothing, sent for her. They wished to train her up properly for their son. This is the usual fate of Hindu girls—to be torn from their mothers and given over to the care of strangers. Little appreciated in her own family, you can imagine the very sad lot a child must have among those who care very much less for her than her parents do. The least fault is severely corrected for fear her sins may cause the death of the precious and idolized son of the family.

When Runabai was sent for, her father bought her many rich *saris* or garments and fine jewels and sent her away with twelve hand-maidens who were to wait upon her in the wealthy home of, her husband.   But alas! for some reason the little wife failed to please her new relatives. Her maids were taken from her almost immediately, and she herself was compelled to work much too hard for her years. They put away the nice silk and muslin *saris* and most of her pretty bracelets and other jewelry. Nothing the child did seemed to please anyone in the family, and her life grew harder and harder. It appeared as though they wished to get rid of her and so be able to procure another wife for the son.

Before a year had gone by her food was limited to one meal a day and that only of rice and chillies (red peppers). She became very thin and looked like a shadow of the bright little girl who came so gaily to this home so short a time before.

One sad day, as she was cleaning the house, she saw some bread on a table. Her hunger was even greater than her fear, and, snatching up a piece, she ran off to eat it. Her cruel mother-in-law saw her, and, picking up a stick, ran after the poor girl. She took the bread from the trembling fingers and pushed it down poor Runabai's throat with the stick. The suffering of the child was terrible. When she next visited her own father's house, she begged not to be sent back any more to be so cruelly treated. "But oh! the disgrace to our family!" the father said.

"No, go back, dear Runabai, we weep for you and our hearts are pained over your sad lot. When we sit down to our good food, we shed tears as we think of our poor, starving Runabai. But what can we do? If we keep you here our caste will be broken and the gods will be displeased. Go back, and if you die, it will be honorable." So the little martyr to caste and false religion went back and in two months more was dead.

Do not think this is an imaginary tale. All the facts were given me by an educated Christian woman of India. I myself have known similar acts of cruelty, even to branding with a hot iron. The real selfishness and cruelty of heathenism can scarcely be fathomed. Even the kinder people tolerate things like these without raising a protest. The very love lavished on some has its real root in selfishness. In Christian lands there is a little couplet showing how very near to the parents' heart is the loving daughter. It runs:

A son is a son, till he gets him a wife;
A daughter's a daughter the whole of her life.

This might be changed in India to—

A daughter is a daughter until sold for a wife,
But a son will support us the whole of our life.

For it is this consideration essentially that gives the value to sons. They will, according to custom, feed and care for the parents. How often this merciful usage is disregarded it is impossible to say, for many a case of neglect and even cruelty to old and feeble parents has come under our own observation. The rule,

however, is for sons to shelter and feed the aged parents. The belief about funeral obsequies also makes sons to be desired, for it is only they who can perform these duties for the father. So anxious are the parents for their sons also to have sons that it is known that they will sometimes try to get an unwelcome or barren wife out of the way so that they can choose a better one for the son. This may have been the motive in Runabai's case.

ONE LITTLE WIDOW.

Seven years a widow and then only eleven years old! Widowed at four years of age! How incredible such a thing sounds, and yet we know there is a land where little children are made widows before they even know the right hand from the left. In Christian lands a widow's sad lot is softened by sympathy of friends, the sparkle and joy of existence may be gone, but there is much to live for and a useful life is still before even a young woman. But the shadow—nay, the curse of widowhood has hung over little Sita ever since she remembered anything. When suffering neglect and cruelty, the little brown girl often wondered why other little girls living near her had such happy, merry times, while she knew only drudgery and ill-treatment from morning until night.

One day, when six of these weary years had passed and Sita was then ten years of age, she found out what widow meant. Then, added to the cruelties she already endured, was added the terror of woes to come. The day on which this knowledge came to her she

had gone, as usual, in her tattered garments and with three large brass water-pots on her head, to the great open well from which she drew the daily supply of water for a family of nine people. She was so tired and her frail little back ached so that she sat down on a huge stone to rest a minute before letting down one of the many buckets which all day long were going up and down in obedience to the many demands for water. As she sat there with her bare, olive-skinned arms and feet shining in the warm sun and resting her weary head on one thin little hand, she was a picture of childish woe. Her faded old *sari* had fallen back from her head, disclosing the bare little scalp, for in token of the deep disgrace of widowhood the soft, dark tresses of hair had been shaved off and the hot sun beat down on the small, naked head. Many sorrows had fallen on the childish heart, but Sita was still a child. Her heart yearned for companionship and love. Many Brahmin servants were drawing water near her, singing little *bhajans,* or songs, and looking quite bright and happy in their gay-colored cotton *saris*. A woman, poor, so that she must draw her own drinking-water, but a Brahmin, came near to Sita and the child looked up and appealed to her for help:

"Will you not draw a little water for me? I feel tired and ill, and the well is very deep."

The woman turned angrily and uttered, in a scathing tone, the word "Widow!" Then she burst out: "Curse you, how dare you come between me and the glorious sun? Your shadow has fallen upon me and

I'll have to take the bath of purification before I can eat food! Curse you, stand aside!"

Poor Sita stands bewildered. She has never asked help before of anyone. Too crushed and stupefied to realize her forlorn condition, she has only existed and gone through the drudgery with scarce a gentle word from anyone. This abuse seems to arouse a little curiosity in the child, but she does not answer the woman. Tears course down her cheeks. Something akin to pity makes the woman pause, and, halting at a safe distance from Sita's shadow, she continues to talk to her in a milder tone. She is thinking, perhaps, of two soft-eyed little daughters, who are very dear to this proud woman's heart, though she mourned bitterly at the time of their birth, because the gods denied her sons.

Looking again at Sita, she says: "Why should I help you, when the gods have cursed you? See, you are a widow."

Then, in answer to Sita's vacant gaze she continues:

"Don't you understand? Didn't you have a husband once?"

"Yes, I think so," Sita answered; "that old, bad man who used to shake me and tell me to grow up quickly and work for him. Perhaps he was my husband. When he died they said I killed him, but I did not. I was glad he was dead, though," said the sad little thing.

"So you call him bad?" the woman said. "Ah! no wonder the gods hate you. No doubt you were very

wicked ages ago and so now you are made a widow. By and by you will be a snake or a toad," and, gathering up her water-pots, the woman went away.

The slender, ill-fed little frame gathered itself up and the child hurriedly filled the brass vessels, knowing that abuse awaited her late return. Putting a small bundle of cloth on her head, she raised the huge jars to their place and hastened to her house, since a *home* she never knew. The sister-in-law met the little thing with violent abuse and bade her prepare the morning meal quickly. The child was ill and nearly fell with fatigue.

"I'll show you how to wake up," the woman cried, and seizing a hot poker she laid it on the arms and hands of the child.* Screaming with pain, the poor creature worked on, trembling if the sister-in-law even looked at her.

This was one day. Each of the seven lengthened years contained three hundred and sixty-five similar days, save that now they were growing worse. The last year the child's head had been shaved. When that has been done, but one meal a day is permitted the widow, no matter how hard she may work. Most of the little girls who saw Sita would run from her, fearing pollution. But there was one little girl, who, like a gleam of sunshine, shone on Sita whenever she saw her. One day after the woman at the well had abused the young widow, Sita found a chance to tell Tungi

---

*I have known personally several cases of similar branding, with a hot iron, for trivial faults.

about it. Tungi's answer comforted the forlorn child somewhat.

"No," Tungi said, "there is a better God than that. Our people do not know about him, and that is why I am not allowed to talk with you. I am married and my husband lives in a distant city. If I speak to you, they believe he will die. But in the school where I go, many do not believe these things."

"How can you go to school? My sister-in-law says that only bad women learn to read," Sita answered.

"So my mother used to think," said Tungi; "but my husband is in school and he has sent word that I shall go also until he calls for me to come to his home. Then he will have a wife who can understand when he talks about his books. He says the English have happy families and it is this which makes them so. The wives know books and how to sing and how to make the house pleasant. My mother says it is all very bad, but he is my husband and so I must go to the school. I am very glad, for it is very pleasant there, the lessons and all, but most of all the singing."

So the little bright-eyed Brahmin wife chatted away, as gay as a bird. The fount of knowledge was opened to her—the beaming eye, the elastic figure and the individuality of her Western sisters were becoming hers.

None of these things seemed for Sita. After Tungi went to school the little shaven-headed child, subsisting on one poor meal a day, went about sad and lonely for another weary nine months. When she again saw

the bright face of her little friend, her condition had grown worse. Her neck and arms were full of scars where bits of flesh had been pinched out in the vindictive rage of her relatives, who believed the child guilty of her husband's death. Brutality growing with use had made them callous to the sufferings of the little being in their power. No one who cared knew of the pangs of hunger, the unkind and violent words and the threats of future punishments. Once or twice she had looked down into the cool depths of the well and wondered how quickly she could die. Only the terror of punishment after death kept this baby-widow from suicide. She had heard many things lately, and she knew of a young and lovely wife near by who had become a widow, lost her little son and, unable to endure the cruelties and her wounded pride, had stilled them all beneath the quiet waters of the well. Another widow, too, Sita had grown to know—an old woman, bent and wrinkled, neglected, care-worn and toiling, who was a terror to Sita because of what she foreshadowed to the child.

One day as Sita was weeping by the gateway of Tungi's home, the little child-wife told the child-widow of a safe refuge for such as she, where neither ignorance nor poverty could exclude her—a home under the loving care of one who knew the widow's curse. After many difficulties Sita found this shelter. Here she forgot her widowhood and found her childhood and girlhood. Here, in the beautiful garden, or at her lessons, helping with cooking, or leaning lovingly on the

arm of "Bai's" chair, the blessed genius of the home, she passed away many sweet and useful years. By and by Sita found the greatest joy in love—higher and better than human love can ever be. Later, when a beautiful young womanhood had crowned her, she was sought by an earnest, enlightened young Christian as his wife.

Many of the millions of child-widows never find release from the bonds of cruel custom and false religion. In Hinduism there is no hope for the accursed widow.

CHAPTER VII.

UP COUNTRY.

Bombay people always speak of the stations north on the G. I. P. Railway as up-country, or *Mofussil* stations. The merchants call their patrons from the same region up-country, or *Mofussil* customers. Some of these places are beautiful rural villages and many are large cities, like Jubbulpore, Allahabad and Lucknow. Even in the large cities you will find beautiful drives and most of the houses are surrounded by pleasant gardens and some by extensive grounds, called compounds. In the cool season tourists find these places delightful, and are often quite at a loss to understand why it is considered a cross to live in India. If they would prolong their stay through April, May, June and July, they would be enlightened. While in Bombay, Madras or Calcutta you never have the invigorating cool weather that we enjoy in Central and Northern India, yet at the same time you do not suffer from the scorching heat and hot winds that are the other extreme in the up-country stations. November, December, January and February, in the northern part of the Central Provinces and in North India, are simply delightful months. Sometimes we even have a white frost to remind us of the homeland. During January the *malis,* or gardeners, try to keep a brush-fire burning in the gardens, for there being little or no

wind, the smoke hangs low over the vegetables and fruits and protects them from danger of frost.

In the smaller up-country places the society consists of a few English officials and the missionaries. In some cities there is a large number of Europeans—as in Jubbulpore. The European community forms a town by itself, quite separate from the native city. In a number of stations there are huge barracks for the English soldiers, who are so plentifully scattered over India. A few missionaries are in very lonely spots, where often they do not see a white face for months at a time. Others are in stations where they have no social enjoyments or privileges, even though there may be English officials there. The majority, however, have some society and, in most cases, the English officials are very cordial with American as well as with English missionaries and help in no small degree to dispel the loneliness of the quiet country life. The work, however, often makes even these opportunities unavailable. Very few of the up-country missionaries can by any possibility secure more than one evening in a week to be given to social or family intercourse. There is the bazaar-preaching at about half-past four in the afternoon, which comes two or three times a week, and the *mohulla* preaching, which is later, to meet the laboring people, who are not at home until late at night, besides meetings for the native Christians on other evenings. During the cold season most missionaries live in tents, traveling from village to village preaching the gospel.

Many of them stay out until April, when the awful heat drives them into bungalows, as European dwellings are called. These houses are built to exclude the heat and have very thick walls, very often built of mud and sun-dried bricks. Where the heat is greatest, thatched roofs are common. Although very comfortable during the hot season, these are anything but handsome, making the house look like huge straw beehives, similar to those seen in old-fashioned pictures. By 8 o'clock, or earlier, in the morning, the house is all tightly closed, except those doors which are furnished with "kuss-kuss" chicks. These chicks are really huge outside doors made of a root called "kuss-kuss," which is fragrant when moist. Coolie women are employed to pour water upon them, so that air entering the house through the kuss-kuss will cool the atmosphere inside. When it is 114° F. outside, these chicks reduce the temperature immediately in front of the chicks to 86° F., which is endurable. In places where there is very little wind a machine called a thermantidote is used. This is a fan-like device enclosed in such a way that all the breeze produced by turning a crank is thrown upon and through the kuss-kuss chick, thereby causing more evaporation of the moisture and a corresponding reduction of the temperature inside. In our study we had a temperature of 82°, while outside the thermometer, in the shade, stood at 114°.

Now comes one of the sorest trials of the missionary's life. Not endurance of the heat or one's own health failing can compare with the sorrow of seeing one's little ones droop and fade. Day after day the

MISSION BUNGALOW WITH THATCHED ROOF, NARSINGHPUR, INDIA.

huge *punkahs* (ceiling fans) swing back and forth and, in the darkened rooms, the children play, growing paler and paler. In the very early mornings and in the evenings they go out for a drive in the bullock tonga or other conveyance or, if older, for a walk; but one sees their health and vigor diminishing every day. At night all the beds are carried out into the compound and, if the weather is clear, with the starry sky for our canopy and the beautiful trees for our walls, we can sleep fairly well. Some of us get moon-headaches and have to fasten umbrellas to the head of our light cots to keep off the intensely bright moonlight of the tropics. How vivid we realize the expression: "The sun shall not smite thee by day, nor the moon by night."

So April and May drag their heated lengths along and—oh! how we sigh for the rains to begin. Then the clouds come, sometimes a fortnight before a drop of rain falls. The hot, stifling clouds hang like smothering blankets over the earth, and sleep, even outdoors, is out of the question. Many a night I have walked around the house for hours in a thin white wrapper, feeling as though every breath would stifle me, and utterly unable to sleep until quite tired out with exercise. Within the last few years we have erected a framework on which a *punkah* is swung, pulled by relays of coolie women, who sit far off in the compound at the end of the rope.

You may wonder how these women endure the heat. They belong to the millions of poor low-caste people in India, and in comparison with such work as

carrying bricks in the scorching sun, they find *punkah-*
pulling for half a night or day in a shaded veranda an
easy task. We cannot remake all the conditions of
life in India. We only know in the hot season that we
are strangers and foreigners, barely able to exist under
punkahs, with all other ameliorations available. Many
missionaries, however, come to endure the heat fairly
well and, during the famine, when so many were superintending relief work, the men were out for hours in
the almost intolerable temperature. Then the rains
begin. In many sections the air does not become
pleasant for a long time ; for, whenever the rains stop,
it is steamy or, as we say in India, "very stuffy."

Now the effects of the continued heat become man-
ifest. Fever lays hold on the children. Days of anxiety follow, often terminating in bereavement. To see
a dear little one suffer because of the climate is one of
the heaviest crosses of the missionary. We are told,
of course, of the English officials who come to India
willingly, but the difference in salaries, which makes
so many other differences possible, is not mentioned.
The children can be taken to the hills, ice is obtained
from some large city and kuss-kuss chicks are in all
the doors instead of in one or two. These comforts
accompany the officers and their families on tours, not
to mention the frequent trips to England, which invig-
orate the little ones.

Some parts of the country are cultivated by means
of a simple system of irrigation and the vegetable gardens must be watered all the year round except in the
three months of the rainy season. One of the discom-

INDIAN BUFFALOES BATHING

A HINDU STREET SCENE

forts pertaining to the hot season and the earlier times of the rains, is the scarcity of fruit and vegetables in all the smaller places. Without these the liver will not perform its office in the heat, and fever results. Here again the difference in salary is important, for with a full purse you can purchase from Bombay, Calcutta or some other large city where fruit is obtainable.

In the cold season everything seems pleasant. The weather is delightful. Guavas come in abundance from Allahabad, the place where the finest ones grow. Later, the luscious Nagpur oranges are to be had, while the merchants from Kabul come down with camel caravans and sell dried fruits, dates, raisins, figs, apricots, fresh nuts, almonds, pistachio nuts, kaju nuts and walnuts. At this season vegetables are plentiful, and good beef can be procured. The housewives busy themselves concocting roselle jelly, which is made from a flower, and much guava jelly and guava cheese, besides orange marmalade, lime pickle, etc., in preparation for the dearth of the hot season. The mangoes come in May, when it is hot, but very few that are eatable can be obtained in Central India. From these, when half-ripe, chutneys and preserves are prepared.

The corunder, a fruit something like the gooseberry, ripens during the cold season. Many ladies, when preparing dainties or preserving fruits which they do not wish to trust to servants, cook over charcoal fires in a queer little bucket-shaped contrivance called a *seegree*. Some have a cook stove in a sheltered veranda, and a few are the fortunate possessors of oil-gas stoves.

The cookhouse is entirely away from the house proper, to prevent the heat, odor of cooking and smoke from passing through the bungalow. Almost every door, outside and inside, is kept open, except in the *hottest* season.

Six or eight servants will do the work usually done by one in England or America, and that number will receive about the same pay as the one in the homeland. The people are not accustomed to working hard, and wages are low. With proper oversight and care about the food, teaching new dishes—in fact, good house-keeping—you can have the work done fairly well, leaving the missionary's wife free to teach in the zenanas, for correspondence connected with the work, and, in many places where there are no schools, for the instruction of her own children.

At best, however, life in India partakes of the artificial. The children must be taken to the hills in the hot seasons if possible. The husband must work on alone. Then, by and by, when the health and education of the boys and girls demand it, comes the inevitable separation of parents and children. A settled home-life, such as we know in England and America, cannot be maintained without many interruptions. Yet, strangeness has its fascination, and many people prefer living in India, while in the case of missionaries the work for and among the people grows to be their life-purpose and interest. The homeland, though enshrined in memory with all its dear associations, still fades and fades away. The one or two furloughs granted are in reality furloughs only, or visits, and

India becomes our home. We are exotics, it is true, but we have taken root. Here we must live and grow, howbeit our life-span is undoubtedly shortened and the burden of millions around us is never lifted from our hearts.

INSECT AND OTHER PESTS.

In the large cities, especially on the coasts, insects do not flourish as they do in the country places, particularly where the heat is very intense part of the year. In Bombay the crow is one of the most annoying pests, although the swarms of these black creatures are considered great scavengers. The crow is everywhere in great numbers. In the country hawks and kites are very numerous and a great menace to the poultry.

In many places scorpions are plentiful, and little children are in great danger from their stings. A child of a missionary died in convulsions in the old bungalow at Narsinghpur from the sting of one which was found in its cap. We ourselves killed one hundred and twenty-five the first year we lived in that house. Its grass roof is a fine shelter for them, as also for rats, gophers and, worst of all, for the destructive white ants. This and many similar houses are eaten through and through by these annoying pests. The walls of many of the older European buildings in India are built of sun-dried brick and mud, but offer no resistance to the attacks of these *demucks,* as the natives call them. They are as small as ordinary ants, but quite white, while the queen is as long as a little finger. Scarcely anything, wood, leather, cloth, paper, is safe. Sometimes they build little tunnels of mud from the

wall to a chest or cupboard and, before one is aware, the contents are riddled. A case of fine books may be destroyed in a short time.

In native houses of the poorer sort, the bedbug reigns and it requires great care to keep them out of European homes, as the native servants are very apt to carry them on their clothes. During the rains a variety of this insect with wings may descend upon a group on the veranda and cause consternation and flight. Moths, crickets and silver-fish are a constant menace to clothing, but these all fade into insignificance when we have to guard against snakes. The greater number are of the poisonous sorts—the cobra, whose sting will kill in twenty minutes; the garetta, Russel's viper and other species. In our own house and compound we have killed twelve, at least, of these deadly creatures. One rainy season there were four deaths from snake-bites inside of two weeks in our town. All through the country thousands of native people die from this cause, their bare feet and partly unclothed bodies giving many opportunities for the venomous sting to take effect.

Among the most annoying pests are the packs of jackals which howl around the house, if it is near the woods, and which even enter the limits of quite large towns. The howling of these beasts is simply hideous and keeps many people awake for hours. There is no danger unless one of the pack has hydrophobia, when its cowardice is gone and often a fine dog is bitten and must be shot.

Wolves often venture into towns and hyenas prowl around after dogs, cats or chickens, and sometimes the stillness of the night is broken by the far-away scream of the cheetah, or Indian leopard.

Tigers, of course, keep to the jungles. About eight miles from our place there is a good hunting ground for tigers. The officials go out with beaters—perhaps two hundred of them. These now surround a given tract, and then slowly advance toward a common center, beating pans and blowing horns to confuse the tiger. When it reaches the open space the hunters, concealed in trees, fire upon it. If only wounded it becomes dangerous, and many hunters are injured and some killed when they attempt to follow a wounded tiger.

Monkeys are a great annoyance and source of loss to the farmer and the gardener. They often descend upon our premises in numbers, sometimes a hundred at a time. They are driven away by noise, but manage to destroy a great deal in their flight through the trees. In driving into the country herds of deer are seen frequently, but these beautiful creatures do much damage to the crops. Game is plentiful everywhere.

During the rainy season, when trees and grass are green, the country is very beautiful. We make the most possible of this season and of the short and pleasant winter.

SOME TREES OF INDIA.

India's heritage of floral beauty lies in her trees. There are but few garden-flowers peculiar to India, but almost every tree is a bouquet of loveliness at some

time of the year, and the succession makes the highway a forest of bloom and turns the jungle into a wonderland park.

Every morning, as we drive to our work or go forth in search of one cool breeze to last during the parching heat of the day, our eyes are gladdened by the sylvan beauties about us, while we breathe the air filled with exquisite odors from millions of blossoms.

The *neem* comes first. There it stands, in its delicate green foliage, sprinkled over with tiny white blossoms like snowflakes. The odor is a fresh, sweet scent, just suited to the graceful appearance of the tree. This is one of the sacred trees. It was under the neem that *suttee,* the burning of child-widows, used to be celebrated. Beneath some of these trees stone altars are still to be seen, where fair young lives went out amid smoke and flame, while the hideous noise of the tomtom drowned the cries of the victim, often a child in years.

The lordly banyan, covering an immense area, is celebrated all over the world. This tree is called by the natives the jungly *anjir,* or wild fig.

The tamarind has a small, insignificant bloom, but the tree is very lofty and its feathery green foliage makes it a prominent object of admiration. Its exceedingly tart fruit is much prized for curries.

The *jamon,* with its tassel-like blossom, stretches its long arms across the roadway and diffuses its perfume, like that of the azalea, far and wide. The light-yellow and green tassels make a great show.

The *peepul* has no visible bloom, but its white trunk and branches gleam through its glossy leaves, rivaling the birch in beauty. In size, the peepul far surpasses the birch. Under this tree we see many idols. Often the bark and wide-spreading roots are daubed with red, and many stop to worship the god of the tree.

The *kautchnor* has a large, white, lily-like bloom, one petal being of a pinkish purple. The flower comes before the leaves, and rows of these trees, interspersed with the fragile, pale-green *sesum,* hanging full of yellow-winged seed, make a pleasing vista of the highway.

A certain road near us is lined on either side for a distance of three miles with clumps of graceful bamboo, alternating with *sesum* and the black stemmed *babool.* The effect is lovely. Indeed, these yellows, blues, pinks and scarlets, with the setting of varied foliage, cannot be adequately described.

During the heat of April and May the *gold-mohur* blossoms. Its flat, spreading branches are covered with vivid red flowers. The common name is "forest-on-fire," and really it seems as though the blooms add to the heat of the sun. For truly oriental appearance, no tree can excel the gold-mohur.

Among the timber trees the babool and the teak stand preëminent. These woods seem almost indestructible by ordinary wear. In the oldest Buddhist temple in South India you can see some teakwood that has endured exposure for over twenty centuries. This temple is situated about forty miles from Poona and is known as Karli Cave, being a rock-hewn structure.

The date of the building is placed as early as 300 B. C., and by no authority later than the beginning of the Christian era. In the great arch overhead, cut in the rock, there are set wooden groins stretching from the pillars on either side. The wood is in a good state of preservation, and but few flaws can be seen from the rock floor.

The mango is one of the handsomest trees, comparing with the hardwood maple in shape and beauty. But the mango never drops its oblong leaves—and, whether standing only in its robe of green or when covered with countless yellowish flowers, or bending beneath the golden weight of the most delicious fruit in the world, it is always a joy to the sight.

Not only in trees notable for beauty or valuable for timber, but in fruit trees, also, is India rich. The mango comes first for excellence of fruit. Then there is the tree which bears the huge prickly jack fruit, weighing from sixteen to twenty pounds. This fruit does not rank next to the mango, but the tree is shapely and prominent, while the more excellent custard-apple grows on a small, scrubby tree.

The good fruit, with the exception of the mango, grows on the less pretentious trees. The orange, pomelo, fig, peach, mulberry and papita are all of small size. There are many other fruit trees. Some fruits, as the *bher* fruit, are very attractive to the black-faced monkeys.

In and out among these trees winds the thread of India's religion, tragedy and romance. Nearly every

tree or shrub enters in some way into the daily life of the people, down even to the adored *tulsi* plant, found in the smallest yard.

Some are prized for their medicinal properties, some revered for their connection with the history of the gods, and some for both reasons combined. This is especially true of the neem. Its bark and leaves are used for healing, and many religious rites are performed under its branches.

As among heathen nations of Bible times, you may find here "high places," or places of worship, under every green tree.

Under these bright skies, beneath the protecting shadows of the banyan and the velvety pink and green of the *chewulloo,* and amidst other beauties of river, hill and plain, flourish ignorance, superstition and heathen rites, proving that mountains, of themselves, do not give birth to nobility, nor do scenery and verdure alone create poesy. While these groves may perhaps produce a single poet, yet from them come thousands of loathsome, ash-covered fakirs and millions of superstitious people who revere these same fakirs as little less than God.

Amid these lovely scenes we long to see the men and women grow into stalwart forms akin to the physical strength of their loved peepul; to behold them putting on spiritual life, as the neem its sweetness and purity; and, to carry the simile further, bringing forth fruit unto life eternal, like the abundance of the rich mango of their groves and plains.

A WEEK ON THE NARBUDDA RIVER.

Camping on the banks of this river during the Burman Fair, or *Mela*, is full of interest to a foreigner.

As I sit writing in the tent, I wonder if more perfect weather could be found. There is a cool breeze blowing and the sky is bright and clear. Winter in India! The time when tourists come sightseeing, and then go back to tell of the luxuries that Europeans enjoy in this favored land; of fresh peas for Christmas dinner; oranges, pineapples and other fruits in abundance; a perfect climate, and so on. In fact, even residents forget the scarcity of good things in April and May; the hot blasts as from a furnace, which seem to dry up the very juices of the body, and all the other miseries of the hot season, including scorpions, centipedes and snakes.

It is in this favored cool season that the great Mela at Burman is held. Burman is a small collection of thatched huts of no consequence except for its numerous temples, its fine bathing ghat, and above all, its situation on the blue Narbudda, which in sanctity is considered second only to the mighty Ganges. Here thousands of pilgrims come every year to worship their favorite god or gods, out of the "gods many" which are here enshrined. Here also come other thousands to sell fruit, flowers, grain for temple-offerings, and all sorts of foodstuffs, brassware, cloth, jewelry and trinkets. Often the number reaches a lakh and a half, or one hundred and fifty thousand. This year, on ac-

MARBLE ROCKS ON NARBUDDA RIVER, NEAR JABALPUR.

count of short crops, the number of people is smaller, probably about eighty thousand. The river bed at this place is very broad, and in the rainy season is often full. Now the river occupies the center of the bed, leaving a wide, sandy beach on one side several hundred yards back from the water. There the land rises in abrupt cliffs which are adorned by small white Hindu temples. Along the edge of this cliff, on the south of the river, are the tents of the English officials of the district, out on the Queen's business, and the more modest outfits of the missionaries, who are on the King's errand among this multitude. Scattered here and there among the trees are the improvised kitchens of the various camps, presided over by dusky-faced cooks, and presenting at night, with the curling smoke from the fires and the flitting dark figures, a fantastic picture. The Fair itself is on the sandy beach below, a small part straggling over the temporary bridge of bamboo to the other side of the river and extending along the north bank as far as the ghat.

This bamboo bridge is rebuilt every year, after the rains, and toll is collected during the eight or nine months to pay for the rebuilding of the bridge and to meet the government tax of twelve thousand rupees. The ox-carts, people and horses may cross the bridge, but the camels and elephants must wade the river a little below, where it is shallow.

From the cliff, where we are camped, the whole animated scene on the sands can be viewed. The beautiful Narbudda seems like two streams as it flows around a small island, green with trees and foliage and

crowned by a little minareted temple. The thousands of pilgrims on the sandy beach, clad in the varicolored garments of the Orient, red, yellow, purple, white and blue, gleaming in the bright Indian sun; the long rows of canvas-covered shops; the booths made of the branches of trees, calling to mind the old Jewish feast of tabernacles—all combine to form a picturesque and thoroughly Eastern scene.

Just where the stream unites below the island, on the north bank and almost facing our cliff, is the magnificent bathing ghat, built of dark stone and consisting of seventy-three steps, each one foot in height. This open-air stairway, over four hundred feet wide, beginning high up on the bank and descending beneath the water's edge, is an imposing sight. When covered from top to bottom with throngs of pilgrims, swaying to and fro, up and down, all intent on worship and praise and prayer, it is a touching sight as well.

Here and there on the stairs are wide platforms. On these small stone houses are built, partitioned off into cells and forming the rainy-weather refuge of the fakirs, or begging priests.

On one of the platforms, bowing before an image too loathsome to describe, is a group of noble-looking men. These are followed by a detachment of the commoner folk, forming the bulk of the throng. Near by is a group of women surrounding an image of the sacred bull; a little farther on a circle of dancing-girls, singing their weird songs, which sound like weeping, and the sadness of the strains seems to tell of centuries of oppression and darkness.

On either side of the river, scattered up and down the banks and on the little island, are the various temples dedicated to Vishnu, Siva, the indescribable Ling, and dozens of others. In and about these temples and on the platforms of the ghat, are idols of all sorts. Some are decidedly indecent and give the keynote to the degradation of the people. A constant stream of men and women is going up the paths to the temples, carrying their offerings of fruit, flowers, grain, sandal-wood, oil and butter; another stream of people, returning from their worship, is coming down.

Much that is meant for gaiety is going on, amusement as well as business being combined with religion in this yearly feast. Merry-go-rounds of primitive pattern; side-shows, where trained parrots and sparrows may be seen, and street-musicians with their long-drawn strains, enliven this bazaar.

One of the most noticeable features of the Mela is the swarm of fakirs. Many of them are dressed in flowing skirts and fancy head-gear, others are almost entirely naked, with their bodies smeared with the ashes from burnt cow manure, these ashes being considered especially sacred and purifying; some are attired in the holy saffron-hued garment, their faces tinted to match, and wearing long strings of prayer beads made from a rough brown nut; others are burdened with an enormous weight of chains, and all are considered holy in proportion to their condition of filthiness and general hideousness. These fakirs are, next to some of the idols, the most revolting sight to a stranger.

may went up from the fair and confusion reigned, as
the shopkeepers endeavored to save their goods, and
thousands who were utterly shelterless ran distractedly
here and there.   The next morning the roads were
full of carts, people on foot, donkeys, long camel
trains and elephants leaving the fair.   Closely covered
wagons conveyed away the few purdah women who
had ventured to the Mela.   Two days later the last
tent on the cliff was folded and, like the Arabs, we
"silently stole away."

CHAPTER VIII.

BEHIND THE PURDAH.

Among the better classes in India women can only be reached by women. The male missionary can never, except by hearsay, gain any knowledge of the women kept in purdah, or, as they say in South India, the gosha women. Purdah means curtain, and the idea is that the women are restrained in concealment or, secrecy. These women are never seen, for when they go out for a drive it is in carriages with Venetian blinds, or with "chicks" hanging at door or window; or, perhaps in a bullock-cart, over the frame of which a heavy blanket or quilt is thrown.

Let me introduce you to two or three of these houses, where dwell zenana, or purdah women. Zenana means simply the women's quarters. Some time ago I saw an article written by a missionary in which reference was made to zenana work. It was written as if the work were done in a country by that name, and he spoke of the people as "Zenanese." While appreciating the ridiculous mistake he made, yet I could but think that the women of the zenanas really constitute a distinct people—veiled and hidden.

But as I said, let us visit a few of these houses. Here is one occupied by a well-to-do pleader. It is a small, whitewashed house with a neat little veranda

in front.   Here the men are sitting and much business
is being transacted, besides plenty of visiting and gos-
siping.   We pass through a side entrance, approached
by a little alley, at the end of which hangs a coarse curtain.   After giving warning of our approach, we enter
the little courtyard.   On three sides are the rooms of
the house and on the other a high wall.   This courtyard is paved and is very clean, in marked contrast to
the courtyards of most of the houses we visit.   The
woman who lives here, although not able to come out
or be baptized, is really an earnest Christian; so no idol
or image or even a *tulsi* plant is seen in either her home
or yard.   She can read also and has her Bible and
songbook in Bengali.

This is a bright spot—an oasis in the desert of
heathenism in which we work.   We have but one other
like it.   Very near this pleasant, though shut-in home,
we enter a similar alley, raise another sack-cloth curtain and find ourselves in a very different little yard.
This is a Mohammedan house.   On two sides are narrow verandas; on the others, sheds for the cow, the
calf, the buffalo, the goats and the chickens.   As this
enclosure is very small, not more than thirty feet
across, we are practically in the stable, with all its
odors.   The yard is muddy, during the rainy season,
and always full of litter.   Over an old bedstead or
charpoy, some home-made vermicelli is being strung
out to dry.   It is far from appetizing in appearance.
Four women are present—the grandmother, mother
and two daughters.   The young women examine my
dress and sun-hat; but the two older women leave

their curry-making to listen attentively to the lesson,
only interrupting occasionally to say: *"Thik bat, Thik
bat"* (Good words, Good words). Then we sing.
Perhaps the chorus is swelled by the low of cattle or
the bleating of the kid. On stifling mornings these
surroundings are anything but agreeable; but the
heavenly missionary, about whom we have come to
speak, was born among such lowly scenes, so we should
not disdain them. Just as we are leaving we notice
one of the women giving opium to a child.

The next house we visit is also Mohammedan and
more untidy even than the one we have just left. We
sit inside the house, but, by keeping near the dingy
curtain of the door, we get enough air to prevent
asphyxiation, although it comes from the filthy courtyard. In spite of these untoward surroundings the mistress is the fine lady completely. She is dressed in
loose Turkish trousers and quantities of jewelry, and
would hold herself above work even if she had to climb
over litter to reach her proper position. Oh! the idle-
ness in these homes! Nothing to do and no one to
teach! Feeling superior to menial work, while the
house and courtyard reek with disease-germs and sickness is rampant all about! This lady is soon busy with
the inevitable *pan* box. From the numerous little
boxes in the lower part of the large one come forth
the betel, cardamom, cocoanut, catechu and slacked
lime, with which the delectable morsel called *pan* is
made. The curious knives are held between the bare
toes of the fair one as she chips up the ingredients.
The lime and the catechu are smeared over the inside

of the betel leaf, bits of cocoanut, betel-nut, cardamom and sometimes other spices are put at the top, the leaf is folded together and pinned with a clove, and then passed around. The native women take the whole strong dose into their mouths at once and chew away until their lips, tongue and gums are a bright red. The juice, ejected now and then, is almost as disgusting as that from a tobacco chewer's mouth. We take a *pan* for politeness' sake, but keep it to give to a servant at home, and comply with the demands of custom by eating the seeds from a whole cardamom, which, being covered by nature, we know to be clean.

Now pass into this Brahmin's house. The wife comes into the courtyard hurriedly to say her husband is eating his food and, therefore, she cannot listen to-day. Just then we see this "lord of creation" sitting in a veranda eating with his fingers from a brass plate. He scarcely dares lift his eyes, he is so afraid we may do something to cause him to lose his meal. Should our shadow touch his dishes, or himself, the remainder of the food would be unclean and must be thrown away. We hurry away, but glance back in time to see the wife sit down at a respectful distance to watch him eat, waiting like a dog for the remains of the meal. This courtyard, to a superficial observer, might seem clean. The mud-floored house and veranda have been *leeped*—that is, smeared with cow-manure and water, which is the usual cleanser for the majority of houses here. There is very little litter about, but under the bench where the water jug stands it is green with

mould and the children are not cleanly in their habits. It is in no way a healthful place to live in, as we understand the term.

Many missionaries, in writing of India, speak of the people as cleanly in their ways. Our experience of ten years among all classes of people has convinced us that, in spite of numerous bathings among certain Hindu classes, which are chiefly ceremonial performances, the habits of the people of India as a whole are anything but cleanly, as we understand cleanliness. There are exceptions, and in some houses we can eat with as good an appetite as in our own; but in the great majority of dwellings the surroundings are disagreeable and the habits of the inmates far from neat or careful.

Besides these homes of upper-class Mohammedans, Hindus of various castes, of poor and rich, we have been in some of the finest houses in Calcutta, one of which was almost entirely built of marble; yet in all these the women live inferior, shut-in and, for the most part, idle lives. As their homes, so-called, are behind heavy curtains and high walls, so their thoughts are shrouded by the mists of ignorance and superstition, their hearts by unhappiness and loneliness and their soul denied the light and life of God.

A dark picture,—but no darker than the truth. I often think as I lift the purdah, which is so frequently made of sack-cloth, how fitting the material which shuts in the inmates of the zenana.

Many, perhaps most of these women, do not realize their own condition. Usage throughout long centuries

day, the woman asked us if our Bible told of the same things as our songs, and especially about the love of God. We told her it did and she asked us to read a verse. As her mother-in-law was present and offered no objection, we complied, and soon we were reading and praying with that family.

The husband is in government employ and, after we had been visiting in his house for about a year, he was tranferred to another station. In order to keep his wife in purdah on the journey, he chartered a car and had curtains put at all the windows. She looked forward with dread to her new home, for she said the house rented there was smaller than the one here, "and this one seems so small, when it is all one's world." This woman is in a prison as truly as if immured for some grave offense. Her one crime is in being a woman. For this, she may never wander among flowers, look up at stately trees, see the expanse of the azure sky or the clear moonlight falling upon the earth at night. She may not mingle even in companies of her own sex, except on the rarest occasions. When leaving here, she was invited to spend an afternoon at each of three Mohammedan houses. She asked her husband about going and he said: "You may have an afternoon for all three houses, and you are not to be out after six o'clock."

So, veiled from head to foot and seated in a bullock-cart whose bamboo top was covered with smothering blankets, this victim of Mohammed's inventions took a brief respite from her prison. The case of this Mussulmani is not an isolated one. Another woman here

came to a little brick-and-mud house as a bride of ten
and never left it, even for a brief visit, until she became a grandmother. Fortunately for her the rains
one summer beat it down so badly that her husband
was obliged to secure another, in which she now lives.
Probably she will never go out of it until carried to
sleep in a still narrower one in the Mohammedan cemetery outside the city.

Hundreds and thousands of such cases, among
both Hindus and Mohammedans, can be found in India. Life-sentences are common. Some women of
the upper class live in oriental splendor and would
resent the statement that they are unhappy. A few
have fine furnishings and surroundings, rich clothes
and quantities of costly jewelry. But these women
spend their days in what would be to their Western
sisters an elegant prison. Others, belonging to the
classes who believe in reform, can go about a little;
but they have no worthy interests, no taste for reading
and live very selfish, empty lives. One woman we
know bathes four or five times a day, anointing herself
with almond paste and costly oils, using expensive
soaps and perfumes, all to preserve her beauty, which
she worships. Her powder-boxes are of silver, her
eyebrow powder-boxes of pure gold, her toilet-tables
covered with silver slabs and her couch draped in dif-
ferent-colored silks to suit the season. Her bath-
room is lined with full-length mirrors and in her possession is every gem except the pearl of great price.
She considers herself a very fortunate woman. It is in
these exercises—in devising new ornaments for her

already overloaded silver jewel boxes and in rich eating—that she passes her days. There is no useful employment, no philanthropic schemes, no real home-making. Even the "eat, drink and be merry" life is carried out in its crudest and narrowest form. The possession of jewelry is one of the chief joys of these women. Even if in common mud-houses, without rugs, carpets, tables, pictures, chairs or any comforts, yet their jewel-boxes will be well furnished if there is any means to procure the gold, silver and precious stones.

The high-class women are guarded very carefully when they go to the Ganges or other sacred rivers to bathe. They go in purdah—that is, in shut-up *garis,* or carriages such as I have described, and usually very early in the morning, before the sun is up, to escape observation.

At some places—as for instance the sacred city of Pushkar, near Ajmere, beside the sacred lake—special zenana ghats have been built by rajahs for the women of their households. The rajahs of Bhurtpore, Odeypore, Jeypore and others have built such ghats there. Above is a court, open overhead, where the women are cutting their hair; or, in the case of widows, shaving their heads and being questioned, tutored and we might add *robbed* by those human leeches, Hindu priests. Then you descend, over steep, slippery steps, down, down, until you reach a room where the sun never penetrates, and so low that you cannot stand upright in it. Here water is admitted for the women's bath. A dark and

dismal arrangement; but, if it is *secret,* it satisfies all demands for the Hindu woman.

One of the underlying reasons for this seclusion is the idea that women are not to be trusted. It is only necessary to read a few of Manu's laws regarding women and some catechisms referring to woman's position to realize what is the real condition of India's one hundred million women, of whom ninety-nine million can neither read nor write. One catechism runs thus:

"Question—What is the gate to hell? Answer— A woman. Q.—What bewitches like wine? A.—A woman. Q.—Who is the wisest of the wise? A.— He who has not been deceived by woman, who may be compared to malignant fiends. Q.—What are fetters to men? A.—Women. Q.—What is that which cannot be trusted? A.—A woman."

Then Manu says: "Hear, now, the duties of woman. By a girl, by a young woman, or even by an aged one, nothing must be done independently, even in her own house." Again he says: "Though destitute of virtue, or seeking pleasure elsewhere, or devoid of good qualities, yet a husband must be constantly worshiped by his wife."

This is, indeed, her religion—to look upon her husband as a god and to hope for salvation only through him. So inbred is this idea of subjection and seclusion that many think, as one woman said in all sincerity to Miss Stephens, in Madras: "I am not a sinner, for I never even look outside of my house." In spite of this degraded position the women of India

have a great influence over their children and, in religious matters, even over their husbands. It is they who see to the maintenance of the worship of the household gods; they who make the special sweetmeats for *dawali* holidays and who kindle the little lights to keep off the evil spirits; they who instruct the little ones in superstitions which remain with them all their lives. In the case of apostasizing Christians it is usually the women, being less well taught than the men, who soonest go back to heathenism. In a case we knew, a child fell sick. The mother wanted something more to be done and, at her instigation, a fowl was sacrificed to the old Hindu god they had left. In other cases women have been known to hide idols, thinking they may be wanted some time, should the new religion fail.

We see, then, how all-important it is to reach the women; and the zenana work, expensive as it undoubtedly is, and requiring so many workers, is yet the only way to reach millions and millions of women—especially those of the upper classes. We are often told that people in America and England think comparatively little of this work, since its results seem so small, and this feeling is exhibited to some extent by certain missionaries, who have been in other work all their lives and have given very little thought to this. If by result is meant the number of baptisms, then we must certainly concede that there is very little use in zenana work. But as we do not believe that salvation is obtained in the rite of baptism, we cannot estimate the number saved by the baptisms received. We

all know well that hundreds who have accepted baptism in Christian lands, as well as in India, have appropriated almost nothing else of the religion of Christ. Many can truly say with some of the early converts in Paul's day: "We have not so much as heard that there is a Holy Ghost."

Hundreds of zenana women have escaped entirely from the thraldom of idolatry through the teaching of Christ's life and example; yet we know that among some baptized, nominal Christians idol worship is often persisted in for years as it was in the early days in Britain among the converted Druids, and as in Paul's time.

All these things are not to be wondered at when founding the Christian church where heathenism, with all its practices, prevails; but it is certain that, in looking for results, we must seek other manifestations besides baptisms and membership in the church.

It is said, however, that in Lucknow there was no perceptible increase in the Christian community until after the zenana work was opened and carried on for some time. The mothers were taught, the children influenced and many are now Christian students in Christian colleges and members of churches. This zenana work was not even begun until 1855, and not one in a hundred homes is yet reached. We do not know the value that God puts upon the various souls in this complex and confusing world panorama; yet how we are stirred and thrilled when a Pundita Ramabai, a Soonderbai Powar or a Sooboo Nagam lay their rich treasures of intellect and heart at the feet of our Lord.

Such are naturally as richly endowed as their husbands, fathers and brothers, and only need opportunity to develop into cultured, noble women.

As we spend money and time in the effort to reach the intelligent classes of *men* in India, let us be equally lavish in trying to reach their wives and sisters. Teach these women until they will urge the sons to espouse the cause of reform and receive and defend the pure religion of Christ. One mother among my zenana women did that very thing. Doubtless there are more like her. The real results to be sought are seen in the lives of the women, their influence over their children, and, in some cases, upon their husbands. A friend, in writing from America, expressed her surprise that we could enter the zenanas at all. "When I read of such persecutions as met Sooboo Nagam Ammal in Madras when she wished to become a Christian, and which followed after her public confession of the faith, I cannot understand why the men allow you to enter the houses at all." Humanly speaking, there is no adequate explanation of this toleration; yet a partial reason may be found in the fact that the men notice a difference in their homes when the women are taught by the missionaries and Bible-women. One man said to us: "You are very welcome to my house. Since you have been teaching my women there is scarcely any quarreling in this house." Such news spreads and, in the interest of peace, industry and cleanliness, we are welcomed. Many of these men desire their women to learn to be wiser and better and sweeter-tempered, but do not wish them to become baptized

and recognized Christians. This latter would break
their caste and all the consequences of boycotting and
ostracism would follow.

There are many women in the purdah homes who
are living beautiful lives; many who never bow to idols
and have none about the premises. Some outwardly
do homage to idols, when others do, in order to avoid
family strife, but their hearts are not in the ceremony.
They tell us that they quietly say their prayers to the
true God and, like Naaman, the Syrian, pray to be
forgiven as they bow before Ganesh and other false
gods, unwilling worshipers, as was Naaman in the
house of Rimmon—secret disciples, it is true, but in
times of persecution there are always secret disciples.
There were such in the olden days in Rome. Even a
Nicodemus came by night into the presence of Jesus.

Many of these women would find very little difficulty in obtaining the consent of their husbands to their
receiving baptism if it could be administered in the
home by women-missionaries. In some missionary
circles in America and Scotland the plea has been made
for the full ordination of some consecrated women to
the ministry in order that this need in the zenanas
might be met. Chundra Leela, the devoted Bengali
woman preacher and teacher, on finding herself alone
with a dying convert who pleaded for baptism, waited
for no authority from man, but simply and reverently
administered the rite—and who shall say it was not
blessed of God?

What effect will all this teaching of the women have
upon the establishing of the Christian church in India?

CHAPTER IX.

THE IRON BRACELET.

In this land caste dominates everything from birth, marriage, death and religion down to the daily meal and even the direction in which a man's shadow may fall. Yet, with all its minuteness, its requirements are so constantly incoherent and illogical that it is very difficult to recount certain customs and ideas without fear of contradiction from someone who has lived in another part of India and known different peoples and usages. The practice of wearing iron bracelets belongs to some Brahmins and Kyasts of Bengal, and may obtain among other castes elsewhere. In some parts of Southern India a wedding-necklet is worn in place of the iron bracelet, and it may also be of different materials.

In visiting a Bengali lady I noticed some very dainty and beautiful gold circlets on her wrists and took her hand in order to look at them more carefully, when a dull old iron bracelet came into view. I expressed my surprise that such an ugly band should find its place among such beauties, when the owner explained its presence as follows: "It is," she said, "the sign of our marriage and is put on by the mother-in-law, and must never be put off even in death." Many women, ashamed of the disfiguring manacle, have it covered with solid gold, this woman told me, but the

iron is always there.   How typical is the iron fetter of
marriage and, in fact, of the whole condition of woman
in Eastern lands!

An American, lecturing on Turkey, seemed to see
only the golden exterior of life in the wealthy harem,
and painted the lot of its women in glowing colors;
but could he have listened, as no man is ever permitted
to do, to the sorrowful story, seldom divulged to a
foreigner, even though a woman, he would have recognized the iron fetter underneath the gold.

A beautiful English girl whom I met married a
Hindu, while he was in college in England.   She says
that she and her people must have been lunatics when
they agreed to such a marriage.   The man is kind in
his way, but they can never have a *home*.   Equality of
the sexes is a thing undreamed of by an Oriental, unless he is enlightened by the religion of Christ.   Even
then, as a rule, he discerns but feebly that woman is
anything better than a slave or, at most, a toy.   As
women rise to their true sphere through education and
reform, these ideas will disappear; but the process cannot be rapid.

Another instance is that of a handsome young
Mohammedan student in England, who married a
lovely but foolish girl.   On the voyage out he produced the iron manacle, telling her that it was time for
her to know that he had three other wives in India,
with whom she must share his wealth, his *house* (not
home) and his name.   A lady on board the same ship
saw the poor, deluded young bride, weeping herself ill

over the railings of the deck; tempted every day to fling herself into the waves and end her misery.

All over India unwilling, purchased and unknowing brides are having the iron fetter riveted on arms, hearts and lives!

A native lady once said to me: "If you English and American ladies accomplish nothing else in India, be sure and do all you can to break up the custom of early marriage. We must look to you. The Englishmen will make laws when the English women demand them for their suffering sisters."

In this same lady's house I saw a bride of eleven years, decked in silks and jewels and smiling in childish satisfaction over her ornaments. Poor, innocent little thing! In a few months the iron fetter will be riveted and, in the dull drudgery of the mother-in-law's home, the smiles will vanish, and, unless here is one of the extremely rare exceptions, her life will be shrouded in gloom.

Soonderbai Powar, an educated Christian native lady, told me of a great-great-grandmother aged forty-eight. She was a mother at twelve years of age—so was her daughter, her grand-daughter and her great-granddaughter. A cousin of this lady was also a mother at twelve. When called in from play to nurse the child, she would pinch it to make it cry so loud that an older relative would take it from her and the child-mother be allowed to return to her sports.

Often a child of ten is not only married ceremonially, but given to the husband as his actual wife at once. Among Brahmins, girls are usually married be-

tween the ages of three and twelve. Not to be married before they reach the age of puberty means excommunication of themselves and their parents. Many girls are given to men fifty, sixty or even seventy years of age. Therefore, thousands are left widows while still children. Nothing can break the marriage bond so far as the woman is concerned. She can never re-marry. The husband can, however, set his wife aside if she is childless, and for various other reasons.

When infant marriages are the rule, not only among Brahmins, but among most so-called twice-born castes, and even imitated lower in the scale, no wonder the fetter must be one of iron to make it binding, and the widow's fate rendered sufficiently terrible to prevent wretched women from attempting self-made widowhood.

Very little has been done by government since 1891, when the age of consent was raised to twelve years. But in thousands of cases this regulation is not observed, and, since the home of the child-bride is in her husband's family, it will be seen how difficult any prosecution would be. A wife must live with her husband, however cruel or unnatural he may prove. It is left to the discretion of a judge whether, on refusal to go back to him, she may be sent to prison. In Mysore, a native state, an act was passed in 1894 prohibiting marriages of girls under eight years of age and of men over fifty to girls under fourteen.

When the act proposing to raise the age of consent from ten to twelve years was being considered, in 1891, there were large gatherings of native gentlemen

to protest against any reform of Hindu marriage customs. The pundits of Poona waited on Lord Reay to remonstrate with him against the proposal. We were living in Poona at the time, and many and bitter were the denunciations of the bill when it finally passed. The Social Congress met in Bombay in 1889 and petitioned government to protect girls, married as well as unmarried, at least up to the age of twelve. Then, in 1890, occurred the horrible death of Phulmani Dasi, a little girl under twelve years of age. Her husband was sentenced to one year's imprisonment. The agitation caused by this case was very great, and, to prove it was simply one among hundreds similar, a memorial was prepared by Mrs. Monelle Mansell, an American lady-physician, which she had signed by fifty-five other lady-physicians. In this memorial thirteen cases, too awful to be given here, were cited, proving beyond question the charges brought against child-marriage on the ground of suffering inflicted. This memorial showed that "death, crippling for life, torture that would put a fiend to shame," all were the result of this dreadful custom.

Another memorial was sent by eighteen hundred native ladies from all parts of India, addressed to the Queen Empress, asking her to prevent a cruel wrong to which the womanhood of India is now subject. This memorial, like that of the lady-physicians, asked for protection for girls under fourteen. The opposition, strong as it was in Poona, was not so great or so violent as in Bengal.

The fear on the part of the government was that the passage of the act would be considered an interference with the religious customs of the people and therefore lead to riot. The bill finally passed, fixing the age of consent at twelve.

The Countess of Dufferin's scheme of a national association for supplying medical aid to women had a very significant origin, showing that in spite of the degraded position given to woman in this land, there are fair and noble examples of enlightened thought among them.

The Government Medical Department is well equipped and you will find hospitals and dispensaries in almost every town of any considerable size. But as nearly five million women live behind the purdah, and fully as many more share the same ideas as their purdah or gosha sisters, they in consequence suffer greatly from malpractice of ignorant native nurses, doctors socalled, and midwives. They would on no account see a male practitioner and so must suffer in silence.

In 1869 the first woman-physician with a diploma who ever set foot in Asia, Miss Clara Swain, was sent out by the American Methodist Foreign Missionary Society. Later Miss Bielby was sent by the Indian Female Normal School to Lucknow. Miss Bielby was called to Punna to attend the Mähäräjäh's wife. When the Rani grew better and learned that Miss Bielby was about to return to England, she sent all her attendants from the room and said:

"You are going to England and I want you to tell the Queen and the Prince and Princess of Wales and

the men and women in England that the women in India suffer when they are sick."

She meant doubtless that they suffer without remedy. Then she went on to say that she asked for no change in their social condition, but only relief from cruel suffering. * Miss Bielby explained the difficulty of approaching the Queen, but believing Her Majesty was good and gracious, the Rani insisted on dictating a message, telling Miss Bielby to write it small, so she could carry it in a locket and give it herself to the Queen. Finally, through some court ladies, the Queen heard of this and sent for Miss Bielby, listened to the message and accepted the locket. She sent the following reply:

"We should wish it generally known that we sympathize with every effort made to relieve the suffering of the women in India."

The subject attracted great attention in England and, as Lord Dufferin was about to sail for India as Viceroy, the Queen requested Lady Dufferin to do all in her power in this direction. This is the touching story of the origin of the National Association, which was organized in 1885. This movement for reform was hailed by both Hindus and Mohammedans and received support both in sympathy and money.

This has alleviated the misery of thousands of cases. It would seem tenfold wiser to relieve much of the suffering of mere children, by still further raising the age of consent, so as to do away with child-mar-

---

*From Mrs. Fuller's book, "Wrongs of Indian Womanhood."

riage altogether. Meantime, while this cannot be done, we hail with joy these hospitals and lady-practitioners for women.

Not only Hindu, but Mohammedan women may well wear the iron emblem of their married and social condition. The Koran does not forbid women being taught religion, and there is nothing in the Vedas or Shastras commanding the keeping of purdah. Polygamy receives far greater countenance in Mohammedanism, and this of itself is sufficient to degrade their women. Added to this the Mohammedans have imbibed many of the Hindu ideas of female untrustworthiness and ignorance, making the woman's lot harder than polygamy alone would render it. On the other hand the Hindus—in addition to the hard precepts of Manu, assigning to women approximately the place of animals—adopted from their Mohammedan conquerors the slavish custom of purdah, so that, by the association of the two races, the sadness of the condition of women in each is doubled.

A case in Bombay which came to the knowledge of an American lady-doctor, and which she told me, shows the estimate put upon women by thousands upon thousands of men in India. This is the story of the native man told in broken English:

"I get disease," he said. It take many rupees to cure me. Now wife get same ailment. For what you cure her? She is good wife, sixteen years old, she cook for me and my three brothers. Not want new *sari* every year. She go up and down stairs all day, carry water jugs up, never complains. If you cure

for few rupees she can live. If you want many rupees she must die and I get new wife. Maybe not get such a good wife." Comment is unnecessary.

How often, when I have gone into Mohammedan houses (I never say home when I can avoid it, for there is no such hallowed place in India outside of Christ's gospel), I have found the wife in bitter tears. A new wife has been brought home and, in spite of all Mohammedans and Mormons may say, the God-given instinct of the true wife cries out against this insult to her womanhood. Often, when there are grown-up married daughters in Mohammedan houses, the father will bring home another wife younger than the daughters. Two or more wives in a home create untold misery by quarreling and jealousy. It is a struggle to prove which shall be mistress of the house or the hut. In one home I visit, the new wife—a perfect beauty by the way—sits in the sun, eating sweets and pan, or in the shade, if it be hot weather, while the first wife and the mother of the husband spin from early morn till dark to earn sufficient to support the additional member of the family. In another family it was the story of "Sarah and Hagar" repeated, for the queenly first wife managed to make a slave of the second, never allowing her to enter her apartment and giving her only calico, brass and glass to wear, while she, the rightful mistress, was attired in silks and gold and jewels.

How these men manage to find their wives in spite of the incomprehensible purdah system I do not know exactly, but probably by negotiating with poor men

who could not afford the expense attendant on giving their daughters as first wives. Often, however, they are taken from other and lower castes and even then the second one frequently manages to be first in position. Monier Williams says, in his book on "Brahminism and Hinduism", that the women are not unhappy in India; moreover, that they are loved. He also declares that cruel treatment by brutal husbands is unknown. In view of the statements made by the doctors in the memorial referred to, this is an unsubstantiated assertion. An old lady in Poona saw a woman, years ago, whose eyes had just been put out by her husband, a goldsmith, because she had spoken to a man when her mother-in-law was absent from the shop. Dr. Stephens, an American lady-doctor, has told me some awful tales of cruel beatings and brandings that came under her knowledge as superintendent of the government dispensary in Poona. I, myself, have seen poor, noseless creatures run screaming to the *katcheri* (court house) with bleeding faces to try and get redress for the shameful wrong done them. This cutting off the nose of the wife, if the husband believes her unfaithful, is no uncommon occurrence, even if the man himself is notoriously inconstant. We see many such disfigured faces and no doubt some are the result merely of suspicion and jealousy. Wife-beating is most common here, and the wife has no redress. After the remarkable statement by so eminent a scholar as Monier Williams, he goes on to say (I quote exactly from pages 387 and 388):

In regard to women, the general feeling is that they are the necessary machines for producing children

(Manu 1x:96), and, without children, there could
be no due performance of the funeral rites, essential
to the peace of a man's soul after death. This is
secured by early marriage. If the law required the
consent of boys and girls before the marriage ceremony they might decline to give it. Hence girls are
betrothed at three or four years of age, and go
through the marriage ceremony at seven to boys of
whom they know nothing; and if these boy husbands
die the girls remain virgin widows all their lives.
They may be taken to their boy husbands' homes
at the age of ten and may even become mothers
before eleven.

Sir Monier Williams then refers to a law, passed
Mar. 19, 1891, making it illegal for girls to become real
wives before the age of twelve, and he concludes in the
well-deserved sarcasm: "It now remains to be seen
whether this law will become almost a dead-letter, like
the act of 1856 for legalizing the marriage of widows."

We, ourselves, know of cases where brides of ten
are taken to their husband's homes, but if there is any
report given to the authorities, the question is asked:
"How can you prove she is his real wife?"

Then Sir Monier Williams goes on to give further
items regarding woman's status in Indian law, religion
and society. After saying that they are not unhappy,
he admits all the following:

It is true that, theoretically, they are ignored as
separate units of society. It is true that they abstain
from pronouncing their husband's name, calling him
simply "lord," or "the master," or "the chosen"
(*vera*), and they themselves are never directly
alluded to by their husbands in conversation. It is
true that for a male friend to mention their names
or even inquire after their health would be a breach
of etiquette. It is true, too, that their life is spent

in petty household duties, in superintending the family *cuisine,* in a wearisome round of trivial acts. It is even true that in religion they are theoretically placed on the same level as Sudras. They are allowed no formal introduction into the Hindu faith, no investiture with the sacred thread, no spiritual second birth. Marriage is to them the end and aim of life, and the only medium of regeneration. No other purifactory rite is permitted to them. They never read, repeat or listen to the Veda. Yet, for all that, the women of India are the mainstay of Hinduism.

Again (page 388) :

Of course, those women of the upper classes who are cooped up behind purdahs, in secluded apartments, vegetate in profound ignorance of the world around them, while the duty of training and forming the character of their children is, I fear, neglected by all. Still, the women of India are generally satisfied with their position and desire no change.

Is there any foothold for happiness in such a life? Neglect the duty of training their children! What would be expected of a mother in Western lands, to whom all the fountains of knowledge, respect and even religion were closed, in regard to training her children? You cannot teach Euclid before you learn addition.

As viewed by a woman's eyes, in rich and poor homes, among high and low, a woman's life in India seems a most piteous thing—a wrong crying out to God and humanity for redress! In the narrow and dingy houses, without music, pictures or books—except in the few houses where reforms are dawning—without social privileges, with no companionship from husband or sons, who despise her enforced ignorance, deprived of her daughters while they are yet little children, eating the leavings of the two daily meals, flying

from the presence of the lord and master—always under the ban of restraint and silence—verily the iron bands on the arms of the Kyast Bengali women are typical of the bands on all their sisters in India!

Prisoners of custom and superstition, they look with suspicion as well as with envy on their happy sisters from the West, and wonder how they can be good and free at the same time. Sitting idle, yet weary—some few in gilded cages, but with the iron hidden under gold, and all crushed by the Hindu and the Mohammedan opinions and rules regarding their sex—with sad, appealing eyes they look to us for light.

Oh! queens of cottages or mansions in the Western lands, honored by your husbands, reverenced by your sons, with fair daughters growing up into noble womanhood about you, turn your hearts, your thoughts and your efforts to your sisters of the Orient. Can you not, like the little Rani of Punna, send a message in a golden locket of love that will open some door, rend some purdah, or let in one ray of light on your sister with the iron bracelet?

A GROUP OF COMMON PEOPLE.

Chapter X.

CHAPTER X.

LOWER CASTE WOMEN.

The question was asked at a large assembly of missionaries in America: "To what extent do male missionaries and native preachers secure the conversion of native women? And what have they to do in training native Christian women in Christian doctrine and life?"

It is easier to answer the second part of the question first. In so far as the native Christian women attend the preaching and praying services, they have the same opportunity of being taught as women in other lands, but herein lies the difficulty. Very few will go to the public service willingly unless they have been pupils in the mission schools, or are wives of workers in the mission. Among village Christians it is well known that the women are behind the men in knowledge of Christian doctrine and life. This is very easily understood and explained. The missionary, or native preacher, can secure but few women hearers as he goes about proclaiming the gospel message. In many villages the women are afraid of a European and will flee from one. A white-face terrifies village children who have never seen such pale features before; and, in a measure, this fear is shared by the women.

The seclusion in which by far the greater part of the upper and middle class women are kept has a reflex ac-

then was only rewarded by the pundit's absconding without giving her a book or another lesson. The family were vexed about the rupee and stopped her lessons for a year. Some of this family were assisted with work during the famine of 1897 and that gave them some confidence in the Christians; so we have permission to teach this woman and three of her neighbors, who have become ambitious through her example.

Another morning go with me and my helpers to visit some sweeper and Basor families. We set a special day aside for visiting these people, as we may not go from the out caste houses into any Hindu or Mohammedan dwellings, unless we have previously gone home and bathed and changed our clothing. These people seem indeed out-castes and forlorn. The sweepers are the scavengers and clean away all sorts of refuse and filth. Most of them have a disagreeable odor about them, and usually live in the most disagreeable and unwholesome parts of the town and villages or, very often, outside of the town limits altogether. The Basors, at least in this part of India, seem a more degraded people than the sweepers, and live more filthily. The houses are mud or grass huts. We crawl under a sort of veranda, not four feet high, and take our seats on the mud floor. Near our feet two or three frightful black Indian hogs are wallowing. One of the women is cleaning wheat and two others are grinding at the mill. A few from neighboring huts come up as we sing. As we read and explain, the women often interrupt by quarreling with one another

A GROUP OF SWEEPERS.

Tenth Chapter.

or throwing stones at pigs and goats. We wonder, as we close the book, if we have not in a double sense been casting our pearls before swine.

But a leper woman, standing as near as she dared, has heard of the healing of the "ten." Another woman says that this visit is her one joy, and she repeats over and over in Hindi the sweet words of John 3:16, so as to be able to say them by herself. She can only repeat, without prompting, "For God so loved." As we think of this ignorant seeker and the poor leper we try to forget the swarms of flies, the heat and the sickening sights that we cannot even write about, and return to the mission-house, unable to eat the late breakfast after the experience of the morning, and thinking sadly of the needs of the poor and ignorant about us. Many writers concerning India note the erect carriage and fine appearance of the coolie women. It is true that the custom of carrying head loads conduces to an erect bearing, but there is very little beauty to be observed among the lower classes. Some of the children are naturally pretty, but most so neglected that they have no chance to be attractive. In the mission-schools you will see many interesting and some even beautiful faces belonging to the lower castes, but here there is care, proper food, instruction and love. The only conspicuous beauty I have seen in India is among the higher classes. Here, again, many otherwise pretty faces, as regards form and color, are spoiled by the dull expression of ignorance or of those imprisoned. The most beautiful woman that I have ever seen, however, is in India. She is a fair Bengali and has been quite well

educated in a mission school. She was lately married and, although her father is a professional man and calls himself a Christian, he married his daughter to a caste-man and she will pass her days in the dull zenana. Her beauty, which would grace a court, and her intellect are hid away forever.

A French lecturer, in speaking of the condition of the American women, said that if transmigration were true and he had the opportunity of asking the fates what his condition should be when he should return to this world, he would shout and plead with all his power: "Oh! make me an American woman!" So, on the contrary, if I had the privilege of asking what fate of all others I would avoid, I should say to be born in India and a woman!

A FAMINE SUBJECT.

CHAPTER XI.

FAMINE.

During the ten years we have lived in India we have witnessed the ravages of two famines. The one in 1896-97 was extremely severe in Central India, and our station, Narsinghpur, was one of the four places most afflicted. To a person in Western lands it is almost impossible to convey an adequate idea of an Indian famine. At the best of times there are so many wretchedly poor people that, to a newcomer from America, it would seem to be always famine here. Thousands upon thousands—nay, even millions in India never eat more than one poor meal a day. Let the crops fail for two seasons, as in 1893-96 and gaunt famine stalks over the land. The old and infirm die, the able-bodied walk long distances to obtain work and the dead and dying are everywhere. The numbers afflicted are so vast that thousands of helping hands are needed to save even a small portion of the afflicted. Orphans swarm in the bazaar and beg piteously for bread, while shut-in high caste, but poverty-stricken women die quietly rather than venture forth.

In 1896 prices of foodstuffs rose higher and higher; beggars increased; there was no work in the fields and soon people began to come in from remote villages to the official centers of districts, hoping the sirkar (government) would help them. The distress increased,

ficials gave me clothing to distribute, as my zenana work made me acquainted with many homes where men could not go to inquire the needs.

Our mission-school of forty or fifty boys soon increased to sixty-five, and then we were full. We rescued almost one thousand children in our own compound and sent detachments to the various schools that asked for them. We looked for a more commodious place in order to enlarge our school and keep the children in their own part of the country. A strong, beautiful building stood nearly opposite our humble school and meeting-place. It was called the "palace" or, in Hindustani, the mahal. It belonged to a petty rajah, who lived some miles away on his estate. He did not seem to care to live in his town-house, and the building had been used for a government office. The story is too long to tell, but suffice it to say that the building became the property of the mission, and, by the aid of relief-workers it was altered somewhat, additional buildings erected, and now it accommodates two hundred and sixty orphan boys, all supported by Christian people in America and England.

Throughout all India you may find these full schools of boys and girls being taught and trained to become useful citizens, and, we trust, noble Christians as well. During the years when the harvest failed in the fields and the orchards refused to give fruit, this harvest of boys and girls was gathered in, and we believe the fruit of these schools will enrich India for centuries.

During all the months of famine the labors of missionaries were greatly increased. Some succumbed to the strain and yielded up their lives in the rescue-work. Starvation was not the only horror, for there were many loathsome diseases which were the result of bad and insufficient food. Many people ate leaves, grass seeds and weeds. Some were even seen to sort out undigested grain from the manure of animals. Dysentery, diarrhea, *cancrum-oris* or famine sore-mouth, rickets and ulcers were all about us. We used quarts of salve and ointment, besides other remedies; still the death-rate was very high. Nearly all the cases of *cancrum-oris* proved fatal, but we have a fine looking Brahmin boy who survived the agonies of this disease and is now a healthy lad, full of fun and mischief and learning well at school. His teeth were loose in his jaws and he used to beg me to have them all out, so they would not pain him so badly.

The suffering during a famine cannot be fully described. The home papers were full of pictures and accounts, and generous friends sent money and food and thousands were saved. But oh!—the thousands who suffered and died!

During the famine of 1900 cholera and plague added their terrors in the same districts where the severe scarcity prevailed. In the other famine, plague was raging; but not in those parts of the country devastated by famine. The missionaries assisted nobly in caring for the sick and disposing of the dead. This latter task Hindus and Mohammedans fled from. One missionary personally superintended the burning of

seven thousand bodies of those who had died of cholera and starvation, and indirectly assisted at four thousand more burnings. Sometimes in this work he found living people being carried off in the carts with the corpses. The stolid driver, on being expostulated with, merely replied that they would be dead in a few hours and, by taking them now, he would be saved another trip. Sometimes a little muscular Christianity was necessary to make the man give up his living freight.

This sounds too horrible for belief, but I heard the missionary tell the incident myself. Not less awful was the shameless cheating that went on in many of the relief-camps. When millions are to be helped the work must be subdivided many times. Some of the inferior officials who had charge of the kitchens mixed fine earth with the flour in order to keep back part of the amount allowed; many gave much less than the regular allowance; milk was watered and other tricks resorted to in order to make profit over and above their wages. Accustomed to look upon the low-caste and the poor as the rightful prey of those in power, these men could easily extend this doctrine until they were ready to seek their own advantage at the expense of the lives of some of their own caste people.

Unnecessary fines were imposed upon relief-workers and never reported, the sums thus gained finding their way into the pockets of overseers. Some of these shameless officials afterwards actually referred to their gains. In Galveston, Texas, martial law was proclaimed at the time of the awful flood. Human ghouls found pillaging were shot down—but who was to detect these

clever swindlers? The poor, famished relief-workers were afraid to breathe a complaint lest they should lose the pittance they were receiving. If, by accident, injustice had been discovered, prosecution would have been almost impossible, for the wretched wronged ones themselves would have been too timid to witness against their oppressors.

What, to such men, were the lives of their poor fellow-creatures? Mahatmas and Sadhus and all their followers know nothing of extending the helping hand to a brother in need. Nay, they do not comprehend the doctrine of brotherhood.

Perhaps the most heartrending sight seen during the famine was that of a little baby trying to draw nourishment from a dead mother's breast. Yet there were even more heartrending things to know about. When mothers offered little girls for sale, and one dared not do such an illegal thing as buy them, we knew some wicked person would nevertheless purchase them for immoral purposes. One mother tried to persuade me to promise three rupees for a beautiful little girl. I did all I could to induce her to give her child to me, intending to assist her afterwards, but I dared not bargain for it.

"What would you do with the three rupees?" I asked the woman.

"Why, eat all I wanted for two or three days and then go drown myself in a well," she said.

A wealthy Mohammedan bought the child, and the mother kept her word.

The Hindus and the Mohammedans do not enjoy seeing the children gathered into the Christian orphanages. Unwilling themselves to stretch forth a helping hand, they dislike to see the children cared for by Christians, knowing full well what such aid means for the future. One native official had been told by the highest English authority in the district to give forty boys and girls from the poorhouse to a missionary who had asked for them, provided the children wished to go. He tried to forstall the missionary by asking each Hindu child, in an undertone, "Do you wish to go with the Padre and eat cow meat?" But to a Mohammedan boy or girl the crafty fellow would say: "Do you wish to go and eat pork?" In this way he succeeded in intimidating some.

Many stories were circulated intended to terrify the people and excite them against the Christians. Some were actually made to believe that the missionaries took out the children's eyes to make medicine from them. Doing nothing, and caring not at all themselves, they would fain prevent the missionaries also in the work of rescue. Many widows and deserted wives were taken in and given homes and taught some useful employment. Thousands of homes were broken up and villages deserted. The very landscape tells the story of desolation. Beautiful trees have fallen or stand bare and dead in the path of gaunt famine. Gujerat, called one of the garden-spots of India, is a dried and bleak-looking waste.

Thousands are praying, some to dumb idols of wood and stone, some to the living God, that the early and

GROUP OF FAMINE CHILDREN AND NINE WOMEN WHO CARED
FOR THEM IN GOVERNMENT POOR HOUSE.

the later rains may not fail again and that India may
never more be visited by this awful affliction. Many
say it is because of India's gross wickedness that she
suffers thus. But oh!—the little children, the young,
young children crying for bread! May a merciful God
stay this sore affliction!

STARVATION IN THE ZENANAS.

Most people suppose that all the "purdah women"
—that is, high-caste women who are shut-in or secluded—must be well-to-do. This is a mistake. A
beggar may be a Brahmin, who, while asking an alms
of you, yet religiously despises you as the off-scouring
of the earth. Moneyed aristocracy has no place here.
A man may amass a fortune and live like a prince, but
if born low-caste he is still low-caste. In a little hovel,
screened from view by a coarse piece of sacking hung
in the doorway, may live a high-caste woman, "born to
the purple" in Hindu society, but so poor that she is
wasted to skin and bone from lack of food. Such a
one said to me:

"One meal a day of plain rice, Mem Sahib, and
often not that. My husband has no work since the
famine and my little baby died because I had no milk
to give it."

Another asked us to talk to her from behind a
door. "I am nearly naked, Mem Sahib. All the
clothes have been sold to buy food. The stomach cannot go empty, even if the back must go bare."

When I took the clothing sent from England for
these women some even cried with joy, they felt so bit-

terly ashamed to be seen in the rags to which they were reduced. To carry grain to these homes was very hard work. Some was given out by government; but, considering the difficulty of men finding out the condition of these secluded women, you will see how hard it was to reach them with help. Only women could really do this work. In the stress of famine many were allowed to go out of their homes, provided they went where women only were to be seen. Knowing this, two of us made the attempt to give out American grain in the back yard of one of my Bible-women's houses. We let in a few at a time and measured to each a certain number of quarts of corn and beans. We soon realized the difficulty of dealing with the poor, famished creatures. We could not let them out again until all had been served and what a scene of confusion that little muddy yard presented! The struggles at the gate to get in were bad enough and, doubtless, we pinched many poor fingers badly as we shut the gate after each detachment of ten entered. Then, if any grain fell, who could prevent the scramble for every kernel? It was pitiful, indeed! By evening we as well as the Bible-women were almost overdone by the labor and confusion. Among this seething mass there were few of the highest castes. Many never complained. Their honor, religion and future life depend on the strict observance of caste. To go on the government relief-work, or worse still, to be fed in the poorhouse, meant the loss of all; so, far better to die and keep everything precious but life! Even without the terrors of caste before our eyes, most of us would prefer to

die rather than to be fed in the government poorsheds, among the sick, the halt, the blind, the filthy and diseased. Some respectable people were there, but respectability was no longer to be distinguished, so wretched had they all become.

Many temptations were in the way of the sufferers. A Mohammedan woman of the upper class was left a widow at this time. She had no means of support; she could not go out to work; she did not know how to do sewing even if any could have been procured for her. She told us that she wanted to live only with her children, but what was she to do? A relative of her husband's sent her word to come to his house as the third of his living wives. This meant protection, food, and clothing for herself and little ones and respectability in Mohammedan society. So she went to the strange town in her long veil and entered the house as another downtrodden moslem concubine.

After money came for helping these women some were taught to sew and coarse work was cut out and given to them from many mission-centers. It was a tedious task to teach these unaccustomed fingers to do even plain sewing and most of the lessons had to be given in their homes, in close, dingy quarters, and often in stifling heat.

When clothing was distributed the applicants, who on the ground of poverty had equal claims, were so numerous that it was very hard to decide where to bestow one's gifts. Most of the women in these shut-in houses live at best in very rough and barren rooms, with neither chairs nor tables—or at best, one unpaint-

ed one—no pictures on the walls and no carpets on the mud floors. There are only one or two beds, called charpoys, with coarsely woven rope across and the wooden part consisting of four poles and four posts. A few cooking-vessels and a rough brick or mud stove complete her possessions, with the addition of a wooden box containing a little clothing and a smaller one for the few trinkets she possesses. This is in prosperous time. But when famine stalks abroad and grainstuffs double and treble in price, the little earnings of the father and sons are insufficient to keep the wolf from the door of the little hut. Often employment fails altogether and the men wander away to new towns in search of work, while the women sit at home and wait, bake their last loaf, drain the last drop of oil from the cruse, and then lie down and die. The little ones wander aimlessly forth to beg or die or sometimes to be rescued by missionaries. People in America often say: "Is famine really so bad as represented?" Far, far worse than any pen can describe! Abstain from food for two whole days; drink muddy ditch-water; eat decaying vegetables; pick up grain around a barnyard and then, on the fifth or sixth day, write your experiences! As bad as represented? Men and women and little children die by the roadside and under trees; parents sell their babies; women leap into wells and Satan's emissaries profit by saving from starvation the prettiest of the little orphan girls. Is all this as bad as represented? Can anything be worse except war, rapine and murder? And are these really worse, or only speedier in their results?

RESCUED FAMINE CHILDREN AT DINNER.

The only relief to this dark picture of famine among
the low and the high is the grand opportunity it affords
missionaries to train thousands of orphans thus thrust
upon them. Some are educated to be teachers and
preachers, but the majority are taught useful trades
and employments, while the girls are prepared to be
housewives and intelligent companions of Christian
men. But the greatest opportunity is that of guiding
so many during their impressionable years to the true
light and life of men. It is not enough merely to save
the perishing bodies, but the bread of life must be fed
to hungry souls, thus to raise up an industrious, God-
fearing community, which may do much to bring prosperity to overcrowded, poverty-stricken India. May
it not be that out of the darkness of woe and famine
shall shine the true "Light of Asia?"

CHAPTER XII.

A COUNTRY WEDDING IN INDIA.

While on a preaching tour in the villages my husband had the opportunity of attending a country wedding and finding out all the modus operandi of marriage arrangements among these people. The son of the Patel (headman of the village) was the child-groom and the little bride belonged to a neighboring village. Seven dinners were given in connection with the great event. At one of these my husband was a guest. The company seated numbered three hundred. All ate from plates made of leaves pinned together with little sticks or thorns. The food was rice, cooked with spices and served with curry—a sort of stew, with very hot and varied seasoning. All ate with their fingers.

The boy was about nine years of age, and of course, it was time to get him married. So, some months previous to this, his father began the preliminary arrangements, or the courtship by proxy. He went about the various villages, apparently on business, but really to spy out a suitable bride for his promising son. He saw many little girls playing about, and, while apparently talking of the weather, the crops and what not, he kept a sharp lookout on the little maids. Some were not pretty enough; some did not appear sufficiently bright; some were not of his caste; some

were of his caste, pretty and intelligent, but of families not high enough in social circles, nor possessed of sufficient wealth. Finally in a village a mile away, he saw a little girl, five years old, who seemed to satisfy the conditions. Her father was in proper standing and had some property. Then followed the usual series of formalities. The boy's father, without saying a word about marriage, slips away to his home, and, gathering together a few of his near relatives, opens his mind to them. They discuss the matter and approve. (Should they disapprove the matter is settled for that girl.) The *Panchayat,* or council of five, of that particular caste are then called together. If they disapprove, this again stops all proceedings. With their sanction, the Brahmin soothsayer is summoned. He also has the power to terminate the affair by declaring the stars unfavorable. The Brahmin reads something from a book. No one understands it and he will allow none to see the page. If the report of the stars is favorable, he says: "Yes, all is propitious, Anoint the boy and girl on a certain day, and on certain other days, give such and such dinners." Then he takes his fee and departs. Next the father of the boy calls the barber of the village and sends him to the parents of the girl. He states the case thus: The boy's parents are willing, relatives approve, *Panchayat* and Brahmin and the stars all agree. All then proceed to discuss the matter, the barber extolling the boy and his relatives. If the girl's parents consent the marriage arrangements proceed. If they withhold their approval the matter

ends. The girl's parents have the same privilege as
those of the boy to take the initiative in the whole proceeding.

The barber returns in great glee if he has secured
the consent of the girl's parents. The news is spread
and everything considered settled. When the anointing day arrives the barber goes to the boy's house and,
removing his clothes, with the assistance of near relatives, anoints him with oil and *haldi* (turmeric) and
then gives him a bath. New clothes are put on the boy,
while the barber keeps the old ones as his perquisites.
The anointing is repeated in the evening by the same
people, but this time it is not followed by a bath. The
boy sleeps in the oil and *haldi*. In the morning another anointing occurs and a second bath.

Now comes the planting of the post. First, four
posts of any kind are set in the ground, at any desired
distance apart; but so as to make a square. Over the
top cross-poles a covering of leaves and branches is
placed. Under this is planted the special post, often
carved and colored in various tints, especially red or
green. The boy has a thin post; the girl, at her home,
a thick one. This post is set by the boy's father, and
the father's sister's husband. In the evening a small
khana or dinner is given to a few near relatives. Similar anointing, bathing and post-planting is also going
on at the girl's house, conducted by the wife of the
barber of her village and the relatives.

The third day arrives and great preparations are
made at the boy's house for the evening khana. Many
broad plates, made of leaves pinned together with bits

of wood, and little bowls constructed in the same way, are gathered in, which have been prepared by the barber's wife. Large baskets, too, from which to distribute the khana, pallao, curry, greens and sweetmeats are being made ready. Toward evening guests from other villages begin to arrive and stop at various houses. This wedding was among the Kirar caste, to which nearly the entire population of the village of Kairua belongs. These have all been invited some days previously by the barber's wife, through whom all invitations must be sent. At about 6 P. M. this same important personage passed around the village saying: "*Khana taiyar hai.*" (The dinner is ready.) The people began to straggle leisurely along. Some remained talking; some finished their milking, or other work. There is no hurry, for they know that not all can sit down at once.

The ubiquitous barber's wife had invited the one Christian family there, and my husband and the native preachers with him, to come to the dinner. They replied that they should be glad to do so, provided no filthy songs were sung and no obscene conversation indulged in. These people think, if these so-called wedding songs are not sung, and this vulgar talk carried on, that the wedding is not at all a success.

About 8 o'clock the boy's uncle came to call the party of Christians. He said: "I have ordered all singing and filthy talking stopped while you are present." They went with him and everything was propriety itself. The Sahib was served first, afterwards the native Christians. They gave the Sahib a little

stool to sit on, but all the other guests had been seated on the ground. The food was disposed of with the aid of fingers only. The dinner was cold and served outside the house under the stars by the light of a few small flickering lamps. The men of the company had eaten before my husband arrived; the women were yet to eat. After a half-hour's chat the little company retired, leaving the wedding-party to complete their ceremonies. With their departure the singing and usual talking began, but in a subdued way. A new idea had been received.

After the women had eaten, the near relatives of the boy's mother gave her a new suit of clothes. Neither the girl-bride nor her parents attend the various khanas at the boy's house, but other relatives of the girl attend. At the time of this big khana a little khana at the girl's house was given to near relatives, and her mother also received a new suit of clothes.

About 4 o'clock in the morning, after the great dinner, the crowd, including the boy and his parents, left for Kacharkona, the village of the bride. The bride received a gift of about 250 rupees' worth of jewelry from her father-in-law. Fireworks were discharged and there was singing, conversation and sleep until about noon, when the guests were again summoned to a meal. Nearly all bathed and then sat down to a great feast. In the evening there was another khana, followed by the real marriage ceremony. The boy and girl were seated side by side, the girl on the right. Then the girl's father's sister's husband took

the corners of their clothes and tied them together, and a Brahmin soothsayer read something unintelligible. After this the boy and girl ran round the post seven times, the girl leading. When they were again seated, a large brass pan was put before them and the guests filed by, throwing into the pan their gifts—two annas, four annas, a rupee, or pieces of jewelry—each one touching the feet of the bride and the groom. This done the knot was loosed by the same uncle who had tied it. The little girl ran into her house and the programme for that day was ended. The guests slept in verandas, under trees or wherever they chose. The next day there was another big khana for them to eat. At this dinner *batassa,* a native candy, was distributed by the boy's father to all the women in the company. The girl's father now presented this new son-in-law with a buffalo cow and calf, a large brass water-pot, etc. On this sixth day of festivities, the guests returned to the boy's father's house, accompanied by the girl, in a *palki,* and the boy on a horse, where he is held by a man riding the same animal. This procession was a noisy one, being escorted by the musicians, who rattle and bang on primitive instruments at intervals through all their lengthy ceremonies. The guests were all gathered together again in the evening for another feast. On the seventh day the boy and girl were again tied together by the boy's father's sister's husband and then proceeded to a *debi* (idol) and poured *ghi* and *gurh* (butter and common sugar) upon it and bowed themselves be-

fore it. Returning to the boy's house, his father sends the girl home with a proper escort and a huge basket of khana and sweets.

This completed the marriage ceremony. The little five-year-old girl was to remain in her own father's house until of a proper age to join her husband. This proper age, so-called, is in India as low as eleven or twelve years, and mothers of twelve or thirteen are common.

When the girl's father wishes to send her to her husband, he will send word to that effect. An escort will be sent for her, composed of the boy's father and some relatives, who bring sweets for the women. Each member of the escort receives from the bride's father a rupee and a piece of cloth. Then the little bride will go with them, taking with her as much khana as she brought home from her first visit to her father-in-law's house. Now she is a full-fledged wife in her husband's family.

HIGH-CASTE OR BRAHMINICAL MARRIAGE.

In ancient or Aryan times, infant-marriage was not the rule, and marriage was not performed until a man and woman were able to live in a house of their own. According to Manu and other writers on religious matters, it was not sinful to postpone marriage until three years after puberty. The young Brahmin, after his initiation or investiture with the sacred thread, lived for several years with a religious instructor and only after his "Return" was he allowed to take a wife and become a householder. The ceremony was simpler than at

present. The grinding-stone (for curry and similar articles) was placed west of the sacred fire and the water jar was placed northeast. The bridegroom offered an oblation and held the bride's hand. If he wished for sons only he clasped (as described by Sir Monier Williams) her thumbs, if for daughters, the fingers alone. Then the bride was led by the bridegroom, toward the right, three times around the fire and around the waterjar. As he led her he repeated:

"I am male, thou art female. Come, let us marry; let us possess offspring; united in affection, illustrious, well-disposed toward each other, let us live for a hundred years." Every time he made the circle he caused her to ascend the mill-stone and said: "Ascend this stone, be thou firm as a rock."

The bride's brother then put melted butter on the palms of her hands and scattered parched rice over them. An oblation of the butter was made to the fire and the marriage-hymn was sung. Then the bridegroom unloosed the braided tresses of hair tied on the top of the bride's head, repeating a Vedic text: "I loose thee from the fetters of Varuna with which the very auspicious Savitri has bound thee." Then he directed her to take seven steps toward the northeast, saying as she walked: "Take one step to acquire force, two for strength, three for the increase of wealth, four for well-being, five for offspring, six for the seasons and seven as a friend; be faithfully devoted to me; may we obtain many sons; may they attain to a good old age." Then, putting their heads near together, both were sprinkled with water from the jar.

The sacred fire was produced by friction of two pieces of consecrated wood called *arani,* and this fire which witnessed their union, was brought by the young couple to their home.

The modern Brahminical marriage ceremonies, for there are three distinct observances, are each complicated and expensive. The initiation of the boy, or his investiture with the Brahminical thread, is followed by a formal performance of the rite called "Return," and he spends no time with a teacher. Two or three days afterward, the second marriage ceremony is celebrated. The little girl, or rather baby-wife, has been chosen for him, and the first, or betrothal-ceremony has already been complied with. Now, at the age of nine or ten, the second, or legal ceremony is observed. Beginning all of these there is feasting and noisy music, followed at numerous intervals by more feasting and music. After all is finished there is again feasting, some wedding celebrations occasioning from seven to twelve grand dinners, with almost unlimited charitable hospitality in the giving out of food to the poor who assemble at the gates.

The real ceremony begins with the night procession of the bridegroom to the house of the bride. Then follows the tying of the consecrated cloth. One end of it is fastened to the bridegroom's dres⁻ and the other to that of the bride's. Sometimes the garments themselves are tied together. The hands of the young couple are joined under this cloth, red marks are made on their faces by ladies of the family, and garlands of flowers thrown over their heads. The red marks refer

to a legend of the gods, too revolting to be recited here and happily understood by very few who use the symbols. The priests then take a sacred cord and wind it round the necks of the bridegroom and bride, joining them thus together while muttering Vedic texts. The bridegroom's hands are then placed in milk and sprinklings of red powder, rice grains, cocoanut milk and water follow. In another room more red marks are applied and money presented by the bridegroom. They return to the first room, where four earthen pots have been placed in the four corners of the tent, most of the ceremonies being performd in a tent or booth erected for the purpose. The couple walk around the tent four times and throw barley, betel-nuts and oil seeds into the consecrated fire which has been lighted during their absence. The priests throw in ghee, and the seven steps around the fire are taken as in the ancient ceremony. This ceremony is twenty-five hundred years old and, with slight modifications and more elaborate ritual, is really the same as observed to-day.

Minor ceremonies continue for eight days. On the eighth the bride and bridegroom go together to worship at a temple—it may be of Lakshmi, goddess of prosperity, or of some other favorite god or goddess.

In all these weddings the wishes of the two principal actors are never consulted, parental law and custom or better, caste, ruling all. Dancing, noisy music and continuous feasting characterize the weddings of the wealthy, which the poorer high-caste families imitate as nearly as they can. Often the savings of a

whole life-time are spent, many rich people spending $50,000 or even more on a single wedding. Woe be to the family whose birth and social rank is high and grand, while their purse is low and humble! To meet the demands of rank, debt is incurred which is often not yet paid by grand-children, for a man not only inherits rank and wealth or rank without wealth, but he falls heir to debts as well. One good result of this extravagance at weddings is that, although, it is lawful for a Hindu of high caste to have more than one wife, the expense forbids it. Hence peace is preserved in many families.

The dancing girls, or "Nautch" girls, sing the loves, quarrels and reconciliations of Krishna and his wives or mistresses. As a rule these songs are most indecent. Many otherwise refined people will permit this, believing it to be essential to the success of a wedding. The jewels and trousseau of the bride in wealthy families are fabulous. In many cases the first order for wedding-jewels is given at the time of betrothal.

The third ceremony of marriage is when the bride's home-coming to the husband's family occurs. Strangers, seeing these processions nearing the house, and hearing the loud wailing of the little bride, are greatly stirred at such a cruel custom. Yet, while there are, no doubt, more weeping brides than smiling ones, it is etiquette to weep and lament at leaving one's father's house. Many brides, immediately after the second or legal ceremony, go to be inmates of their husband's home, even though he may yet be at school or away at college. At the proper age she becomes his actual

wife and—alas! too often at an improper age, for the
rule is in India to blossom early and fade young.
Many boys in school are already fathers. There is indeed no proper founding of a home, no real individual
family life; a sort of common shelter only with individual wives. And where a mother-in-law and four,
five or more daughters-in-law live in one house,
whether large or small, there is usually very little love
or happiness—at best a stolid endurance, at worst
discord and discontent. There may be jewels, rich carpets, silver and brass, but it is difficult to cultivate the
meek and quiet spirit, and almost impossible to capture
Joy in such a household.

MOHAMMEDAN WEDDING.

Mohammedan girls are usually betrothed between
the ages of twelve and sixteen and the marriage occurs
soon after. Some are betrothed even younger. As in
the case of the Hindus, the barber and his wife are employed as match-makers, the man making all arrangements among the men and his wife acting as go-be-
tween among the women of the two families. When
the parents on both sides are satisfied, an invitation is
issued by the bridegroom and his family to their friends
to accompany them to the bride's house with gifts.
These presents consist of two rings, gold or silver, as
financial circumstances permit; a quantity of sweetmeats called *batassas,* a suit of clothes and one rupee,
one anna in coin. The prospective mother-in-law
places five or seven handfuls of batassas, with the
rupee, in the girl's lap. The one anna (worth two

cents) is passed over the girl's head and then given to the barber's wife. Then the inevitable *pan supari* is distributed. This is chopped betel-nut, spices, lime, and catchu rolled up in a fresh pän leaf, or betel leaf and pinned with a clove. This, in India, takes the place of tea, and is the expression for hospitality. Even at feasts it has its place and lends the finishing touch to every entertainment.

After the bride receives her gifts, the compliment is returned and the bridegroom-elect is given a new pugri, a handkerchief, two rings and the one rupee and anna in money, the anna going to the barber.

This gift ceremony is called the *Mangni* or asking, At this time the date is fixed for the wedding, which may take place a week, a month, or a year afterwards.

Before the real marriage there are great preparations at the house of the bride. Fritters of flour, sugar and ghee are fried and rice-cakes and other toothsome things are prepared. The whole night prior to the wedding, servants and retainers are busy cooking and baking.

At midday the *Kazi,* or religious judge, arrives, accompanied by the friends of the bridegroom, bringing gifts of jewelry, brass cooking-utensils, clothing, money, etc.

The girl sits behind the purdah, or curtain, with her parents. The Käzi and bridegroom take their places some distance away, in front of the curtain. Two men, chosen as witnesses, now approach the purdah and ask the girl if she will accept them as witnesses. After receiving a muffled affirmative, the chief question is

asked—whether she is willing to take the man whom her parents have chosen for her as her lawful husband. Again a muffled consent is received, and this is reported to the Käzi and the bridegroom. The witnesses are sent back three times to make certain of the answer. After this is settled the parents come to terms, through these same witnesses, as to what they are to pay or receive in case one of the contracting parties deserts the other. In well-to-do homes this is a large sum.

After this the Käzi reads from the Korän in regard to the duties of marriage, and finally pronounces them man and wife. Up to this time the young couple have not seen each other. In the evening the bride is carried in a palanquin to her husband's house, the bridegroom accompanying the procession on horseback. Native bands and quantities of fireworks enliven the procession. The introduction of the bride and groom takes place by means of a mirror, which is held before the bride's face, the young husband looking over her shoulder. If displeased, he may console himself with the thought that the second venture may prove more agreeable, but for the bride there is no mitigation of possible disappointment.

The wedding garments and jewelry of both bride and groom, among the rich, are quite magnificent, costing thousands of rupees. The gold and silver tinsel and gems which sometimes encrust the velvet coats and other garments make the trousseau very dazzling. For several weeks after the marriage the bride sits daily on a charpoy, or bedstead, for inspection by female visitors. Each one may get a glimpse of her face

where the railway ended. From thence, by night traveling, in an uncomfortable *tonga,* we journeyed to Rajpur. Then we took "dandies," a sort of palanquin, and were carried up the sharp ascent of seven miles. Looking back, as we circled around some sharp curve, we could see the second dandy following below. Sometimes we seemed hanging over an unfathomable abyss. The air grew cooler and cooler. More wraps were donned and at length we reached Mussoorie, or more correctly Mun-suri (delectable mountain).

The scenery was grand in the extreme. One morning I took a long ramble alone around a peak called "Camel's Back." Suddenly, at a turn of the road, with a perpendicular wall on the inside and a fearful precipice on the outer edge, straight in front of me, I saw the distant snow-peaks, dazzling white and tinted with rosy red in the beams of the rising sun. I had not seen snow for six years and, forgetting everything but the glory of the scene, I shouted: "The snows, the snows, the everlasting snows!" It was a moment of ecstasy. Never after, during all the three months of our stay, was the air clear enough for another such view. Everything seems perpendicular in Mussoorie. No horse or bullock conveyance can be used on the precipitous roads. Only dandies, jampäns and jinrickshas are to be seen. There is constant climbing. For children, the roads are very dangerous and almost every year one or more fall over the steeps, sometimes never to be found, as the wild beasts below reach them before the hill-men can descend. A fall of this sort is always

fatal, since the slope is so precipitous that nothing prevents the body from repeated blows until life is extinct.

There are hotels in all these hill-stations, many plain boarding-houses and an occasional mission-sanitarium. Some missionaries cannot endure the climate on the plains for more than a year before they require a short change to the hills; others can remain four, five or six years, while still others never go to the higher lands at all. The children suffer most from the heat and malaria of the plains. Most of the English officials send their wives and children to the hills every year, even when they themselves cannot go.

If missionaries had this healthful change more frequently many lives would be lengthened for service. It sometimes seems as though people at home approve of martyrdom in the case of missionaries, for we sometimes hear unfavorable criticism of these hill-journeys. This is, indeed, martyrdom by proxy. Many here even incur debt in order to get to the hills to save a loved one's life. Come to India, dear friends, and see; but let it not be in the cool season. Be sure to remain through April, May and June. Stay two seasons, if possible, for very few realize the full power of the heat the first season. Most of us find it harder to endure from year to year, as our systems become more debilitated. By the third hot season we fancy all our visitors would also be "going to the hills" and their most ardent longing would be for a glimpse of the snows, the everlasting snows.

portion of Ooty, and it looked as beautiful as human mind could conceive the New Jerusalem in prophet's vision.

Ah! yes, to the hills, to the everlasting hills, weary toiler on the plains of India, and weary toilers on the plains of life! 'Tis true the work, the endurance, the casting out of demons, lies below the mount; but let us ascend now and again and breathe the purer, loftier air of the earthly and heavenly summits. So shall our bodies endure the time of conflict, our minds and spirits remain calm in the tumults and from the other heights of prayer and faith our souls be equipped for further flight, some wondrous day.

PEOPLE OF THE HILLS.

In the Himalayas there is a sturdy, independent race of men. They have little land-holdings here and there in the mountains, but come during the summer months to the health resorts to find remunerative toil. They are a rough, unkempt, dirty-looking people, but their manners are entirely different from the cringing behavior of the coolie on the plains. A lady was being carried along in a jampan by four of these hill coolies. She had complained a great deal all the way, and they finally set her down, declaring she must promise to stop scolding or else pay them extra for listening to her. She prevailed on them to go on after swallowing her pride sufficiently to give a feeble assurance, but no sooner was she on the way again than she resumed her lamentations. They promptly put her down, demanding a fine because she had not kept her word, which, being unable to walk, she was forced to pay. These

men are fine climbers and, having learned how much the hill-ferns in their countless varieties are prized by visitors, they bring them, with quantities of orchids and other flowers, to the hotels and boarding places for sale. They often descend the precipitous cliffs to search for children who have fallen over.

Very different from these independent men are the Gonds, the aboriginals who inhabit the low hills in the central provinces. They are a hunted and down-trodden people. From the early Aryan times they have been used to being beaten back into the hills before the encroachments of the fairer and more aggressive Aryans. They are ignorant and wild, following primitive agriculture as a livelihood and herding a few cattle and goats to eke out their subsistence. Their experience of oppression has led them to conclude that power is always associated with a desire to destroy or maltreat; thus their religion is a sort of devil-worship. They hope by offerings and ceremonies pleasing to the evil spirit to ward off his malevolent designs and so to live in peace. They have a most humble opinion of themselves. When Mr. Lampard went to begin missionary work among them they could not comprehend his motives and suspected him for some time. When they became convinced that he did not mean to harm them, but had come for their good, to teach them about a God who did not hate, but loved even such wild children of the hills as themselves, their astonishment knew no bounds. "Why," they said, "of what use is it to try to teach us; we are only monkey-men. Better leave us in our jungles."

During the famine these poor people suffered terri-
bly. Having only their little fields to depend upon,
when the evil spirit dried up the clouds and parched
the young grain and the grass, what were they to do?
Many toiled on the government relief-works. But
after fathers and mothers had died and the little hut
was gone, with not even a cooking-pot left, boys and
girls wandered into the towns and were taken to the
poor-sheds to be fed, or gathered into the mission-com-
pounds which stood hospitably open. Now, many
dark, rough-featured little Gonds are standing in the
orphanages beside the fair, aristocratic Brahmin boys
and girls who were also orphaned during those dark
times. They will no doubt go back to the hills some
day—but let us believe that it will be to plant Christian
homes and villages and bring the Christian God of
love to the "monkey-men" who now fear only hob-
goblins and evil spirits.

THE TODAS OF THE NILGIRI HILLS.

The great variety of people and languages found in
India is difficult for a foreigner to comprehend. Many
writers describe the characteristics of "A native of India," forgetting that there is almost as much difference
between the Bengali and the Punjäbi as there is between the Spaniard and the Scotchman.

Perhaps no other of the many peoples of this empire has been so little heard of or written about as the
Todas of the Nilgiri hills; yet they are very interesting
and totally distinguished from any other tribe or caste
in customs, worship and physique.

GROUP OF TODAS AND THEIR DWELLING.

To see them roaming these hills, herding the buffaloes they love so much, clothed only in a single flowing cloth thrown about their bodies, one might conclude that they were nomadic and almost wild. But their little groups of mound-shaped huts are permanent homes. These tiny villages are called *munds,* and a visit to a "Toda mund" is one of the prescribed entertainments for all visitors to these hills.

The women and children are usually found alone, with perhaps one or two old priests sitting about. The men are off on the beautiful downs pasturing their herds. A dairy-temple and a buffalo enclosure are found in each mund.

Strangers are not allowed to enter these temples or even to look into them. They are called "dairy-temples" because used for ceremonies connected with buffalo-worship. Great quantities of milk and *ghee* (clarified butter) are used as offerings to their gods, the uncouth animals they tend and worship. The Todas admit that in some temples there are images, but of what sort they do not tell. In some way these must also be related to buffaloes, for all a Toda's thoughts and affections cling about these creatures. All their songs are about the buffaloes, and anything more uncanny than these songs, sung by a dozen or more women with lips nearly closed, is hard to imagine.

The temples are of the same shape as the dwelling-hut shown in the picture. While they would not allow us to enter the temples, we were allowed to crawl on our hands and knees through the low aperture leading into the dwelling. The one we entered we found very

clean and tidy, although everything was well seasoned with smoke, as there is no opening for it to escape except the low door.

Most people admire the appearance of these people. Almost all of them have very beautiful, long, silky, curling hair—even the men—and their bodies are strong and well formed. They are, however, as a people, rapidly passing away. They now number, all told, only seven hundred, and we cannot wonder when we know that the revolting custom of polyandry exists among them. They are probably the only people known who retain this practice.

Should a Toda decide to become a Christian he would find it extremely difficult. His wife he must leave forever, for she is the joint wife of himself and his brothers. Harder still, he must leave what is far dearer to a Toda's heart than his wife, his beloved buffaloes, which are also owned in common by his brothers and himself. He could claim no children, and, with buffaloes, occupation, wife, children and home gone, he would be a veritable waif.

The Todas know nothing of their origin. So far as I can ascertain those who work among them know quite as little on that point. The Todas themselves say they have always lived in these hills and owned their buffaloes. They wear but one garment—a loosely arranged blanket of cotton or wool.

The great event toward which a Toda's thought and care are directed is his funeral. Before the English regulated the sacrificing of the buffaloes there used to be a perfect carnage of the sacred animals. For, al-

SACRIFICING A BUFFALO AT A TODA FUNERAL.

though the Toda worships his herds, yet he uses them
for sacrifices, not revering their life as the Hindu does
that of the sacred bull and cow.   The number killed at
a funeral depends on the rank and wealth of the dead
Toda.   These animals are not in the least docile, and
often in capturing them a young Toda is killed and
then there is another funeral and more buffaloes sacrificed.   There are two funeral services, one being held a
year after the death occurs.   The women sit before the
dead Toda's hut, singing their weird songs.   At ten
o'clock in the day a new hut is built, and in it are placed
the club, cloth and utensils of the deceased.   Offerings
of ghee and cloth are brought and placed before the
hut.   Then all dance before it and utter cries resembling
the howling of jackals, which of all sounds ever heard
is the most hideous.   After this violent exercise dinner
is served to all on green leaves instead of plates.   The
next day the buffaloes are sacrificed.   These are to furnish the dead Toda with nourishment in the happy buffalo heaven to which he aspires.

Mission effort among these people was begun only
eight years ago, and as yet no Toda has been converted.
Miss Ling, the devoted missionary who works among
them, has translated Mark's gospel and some Christian
songs into their tongue.   As they have no written language she was obliged to use the Tamil character, the
Tamil being the language largely used in South India.
Some impression has been made on these people, as
the two incidents following will show:

A woman who had been taught for some time lost
her sight.   She was taken by the missionary to the hos-

pital and was cured. The first Sunday after she left the hospital she came to the Christian Tamil service. When asked why she was there, as she could not understand the preaching, singing or praying, she answered: "I am thankful to God for giving me sight, and He understood all that was said and my heart, too." Her eyes had been opened to the God who is a spirit, or she would have bowed to her buffaloes and thanked them for her sight.

The second incident relates to a Toda boy who had been instructed in a Sunday-school. He had had a dream and told Miss Ling that it made him sad. He dreamed he saw tribes and tribes going into heaven. There were white people and brown and black, Brahmins, low-caste and Mohammedans, and many that he did not know, but not one Toda. Miss Ling answered by singing in his own language, "Jesus, I Will Follow." As she finished the boy said: "I will follow." He seemed really trying to do so. Let us hope that he may continue until he is a man and perhaps help to lead his own people into Christ's light.

To become *Christians* they must cease everything, almost, which distinguishes them as a people. Families must be broken up and Christian marriages instituted. Even their occupation would be a temptation to them.

In some parts of Ireland, where peculiar dialects linger, it is said that a form of the Lord's prayer is still used in which the expression "Deliver us from evil" is rendered "Deliver us from Druidical practice." So these poor Todas, bound hand and foot, as it were, to the uncouth creatures they worship, will some day pray

"Deliver us from buffalo-worship," for they, too, shall ultimately join the ransomed throng here on earth, and, delivered from the terrible custom of polyandry which has decimated their race, become strong dwellers in these blue mountains, praising our God amid this beautiful scenery, and perhaps going now and then to visit the old munds where their ancestors lived in the ancient days of buffalo-worship.

CHAPTER XIV.

ORIENTAL PALACES AND TOMBS.

Delhi is called the Rome of Asia, because it is so full of beautiful buildings and interesting ruins. The old part, abounding in relics of bygone days, together with the new, covers an area of ten miles by six. It is really divided into seven Delhis. Inside the entire area there are seven castles and fifty-two gates. All these, besides tombs, pillars and old Buddhist remains, are extremely interesting.

Delhi was settled by the early Aryans, but the Hindu monarchy was probably removed before the Christian era. Of all the reigns before that era that of Asoka is probably the only one of which we have really authentic history. During his reign the Buddhist faith was proclaimed the state religion and from his *laths,* or pillars, at Delhi and Allahabad, we learn many of the civil and religious laws which he proclaimed. These are known as "Asoka's Edicts" and are in the Pali language. He came to the throne about 263 B. C.

In the eighth century, A. D., Delhi became the metropolis of the Tamar Rajpoots. These were overthrown by the Pathans of Ghazni. Later, in 1193, the first of the slave-kings of Delhi ascended the throne. This king, Kuth-ud-din, having been a slave of Mohammed Ghori of Ghazni, had been made viceroy and ultimately became king. It is probably in his honor

THE EXQUISITE MARBLE FRETWORK SCREEN INSIDE THE TĀJ MAHAL, AGRA.

that the Kutub Minar, the great tower called the pride of Delhi, was built, as its architecture is pronounced pure Pathan.

The Pathan kings reigned until 1556 when, after several dynasties of the Pathans, the Moghuls became firmly established. Baber was the first of the Mogul kings. He lies buried in Kabul, but the tomb of his son, Humayun, is outside of Delhi on the beautiful road to the Kutub. It is of red sandstone and a most beautiful and perfectly preserved building of the early Moghul days. A beautiful story is told of Baber and his son Humayun. The latter was dangerously ill and the king formed the loving resolve to give his life for his son's. He walked around the bed three times and said: "I have borne it away." The son improved and the father declined from that day. The great Akbär was Humayun's son. He removed the capital to Agra. He seems, on the whole, to have been a wise and able ruler, and, judging from his pictures, which you may see at Delhi, he was handsome and noble-looking. His son, Jehangir, was quite different from his father, being given to debauchery and cruelty as well as great intolerance in religion. His queen, Nur Mahall (Light of the Palace), afterwards called Nur Jahan (Light of the World), was very influential and she and her brothers managed the affairs of the kingdom with prudence and humanity. Nur Mahal's history is like that of a fairy-story. She was of a noble Persian family which had been reduced to poverty. Her father emigrated to India. On the way Nur Jahan was born. The parents were in such extremity that they put the infant on the

public road to excite compassion. A rich merchant took it for his own, hiring the mother as its nurse. Through this kindness the family were introduced at Akbär's court. Here Jehangir saw the young and beautiful girl and was captivated by her. His father ordered her marriage with a Persian, Sher Afkan. When Jehanzir became emperor he tried to induce Sher Afkan to divorce Nur Jahan. He refused and, in the quarrel that ensued, he as well as his viceroy were killed. For some time Nur Jahan would not listen to the emperor, looking upon him as her husband's murderer, but he finally prevailed and she became empress of India. Her influence was unbounded and she used it for good.

Shah Jehan was Jehangir's third son. His wife was Mumtaz Mahal, for whom the wonderful Taj at Agra was built. After her death he could not endure life at Agra and removed the capital back to Delhi, where it was before great Akbär's time, eighty years before.

The fortress and palace of new Delhi is said to have cost 50 lakhs of rupees, or more than a million and a half of dollars. In the great hall, *Diwani Am,* the kings held audience for all, arranged by rank. In this hall is a fine throne of white marble. On the left is the *Diwani Khass,* or special hall of audience. It is the finest building of its kind in India, and perhaps in the world. Its sides are open save for rows of massive columns on the four sides. The dimensions are 80x160 feet and there are thirty-two pillars, some large and some small. All have rich, fluted edges and Corinthian capitals. The relief work, and the capitals of all but

the outer row, are richly overlaid with heavy gold leaf. At one end, separating the principal part from the women's hall, there is an exquisite white marble fretwork screen. From a distance it looks like lace; even closely examined it is faultless. Above this screen is a representation of the scale of justice in relief-work, overlaid with gold. This entire hall of white marble, with its superb mosaics of birds and flowers done in precious stones, its frescoed ceiling of fine woods set into the marble, its fluted Moorish arches, is the most ornate, perfectly oriental spot imaginable. When the "Peacock Throne" stood in its midst it must have been the materialization of an Arabian Night's dream. Over the rich cornice of the ceiling is the exquisite motto, in large Persian letters of pure gold.

اگر فردوس بروے زمین است

همین است وهمین است وهمین است

"If there be an eylsium on earth, it is this, it is this, it is this!"

The place is indeed so beautiful with its rich ornamentation and the exquisite vistas of palm and flowering shrub from between the magnificent pillars that even an Occidental is fain to confess it an Elysium and echo the motto, "It is this! it is this!"

The palace itself is a marvel of beauty and richness, nor it is less opulent in history and romance. Here, in 1716, Hamilton, the Scottish surveyor, cured Farrokh Siyar on the eve of the latter's marriage. The em-

peror left it to the doctor to name his reward. He asked on behalf of the deputation from the small British factory at Calcutta that it be allowed to establish a factory and to maintain thirty-seven towns on the Hoogley river. This was the foundation of "The Presidency of Fort William" and all that came therefrom.

In 1739 Mohammed Shah entered the throne-room with Nadir Shah of Persia and the two sipped coffee on the Peacock Throne. The next day the treacherous Persian had the citizens massacred and watched the slaughter from the terrace of a mosque in Chandni Chauk, one of the great streets of the city. He then carried away great booty, among it being the Peacock Throne, all being valued at £80,000,000 sterling. In 1803 Lake's cavalcade filed into the Diwani Am. In 1857 the last of the Moghuls consented to the butchery of helpless English women and children and he himself, the last of the line of Baber, afterward died an exile in a strange land. Chandni Chauk, or Silver Thoroughfare, has lost its splendor, but we saw many costly rugs, much silverware and carpets of fabulous value displayed for sale.

The Jamna Musjid is called the greatest mosque in the world. The minarets are one hundred and thirty feet high and the great courtyard is three hundred and ten feet square. The building was begun in 1644 and five thousand workmen were constantly employed for six years. It is a massive structure of red sandstone. The floor is of alternate white and black marble blocks, each large enough for a devout Mussulman to pray upon. There are no seats, as the Mussulman either

THE METHODIST THEOLOGICAL SEMINARY, BARIELLY.

stands or kneels on his praying mat. We were shown a piece of rock containing an impression of Mohammed's foot, an old slipper of the prophet's; also a Koran said to have been brought from Mecca thirteen hundred years ago. I chose to believe the Koran and slipper myths, but rejected the one about the rock.

As we drove out to the Kutub we saw, from a distance, the Kotila of Firoz Shah, with stone pillar. This pillar is an ancient Buddhist relic, said to have been brought down from the sub-Himalayan country, where the contemporaries of Antiochus and Ptolemy had one of their chief seats. This pillar has stood for ages upon a three-storied structure. It once had a globe and crescent at the top and was gilded. It is forty-two feet seven inches high. Its date is given as 1351 to 1388 B. C. The inscriptions are well-known edicts of Asoka (third century, B. C.), but they must have been inscribed later.

On this same road we saw the great fortification of Indrapat, or sixth Delhi. Inside this fort is a fine mosque of Pathan architecture. This magnificent fortification is now inhabited by 10,000 low castes. Farther on this historic road we saw Hunayun's tomb, built by his wife and finished by Akbär, his son. This beautiful structure is of the earliest Moghul period and was built a century before the Täj. Its dome is three-fourths the size of St. Paul's, London, and is of a different shape to that of the Täj; yet in the marble dome, side kiosques, majestic portals and storied openings and lofty plinth, it was clearly the forerunner of the Täj. It is built of red sandstone and white marble. From its

Near it is the "Iron Pillar of Asoka," said to mark the center of the earth. Under it there is said to be vast quantities of coin and numbers of idols. It is the oldest thing in Delhi.

Ägra, the other capital of the old Moguls, is very little to look at now, as a city. Its ancient glory has departed, except the beautiful buildings which have stood for several centuries and will remain for centuries still, unless forcibly destroyed. The fort is simply magnificent, and inside it is the beautiful palace of Akbär. This is built of pure marble, most elaborately and exquisitely adorned with mosaics of flowers and designs in carnelian, turquoise and other precious stones. The most perfectly beautiful spot is the Jessamine Tower, which was built for Mumtaz Mahal, the idolized wife of Shah Jahan, the "exalted," or "chosen" of the palace. Near it are beautiful terraces enclosed with marble screens of such delicate, lace-like workmanship as to seem indeed the fabric of a dream. This tower, enriched with its mosaics representing the jessamine flower and plant in most beautiful designs, overlooks the Jumna river, which here describes a curve, seeming to enclose the piece of land on which the Täj is built. So, across the water, the beautiful queen would watch the Täj rearing its snowy loveliness to her memory, and in this lovely Sumam Burj, with its golden dome, would dream away the soft moonlight nights, reclining on silken cushions. Truly everything is luxuriant and oriental in the extreme.

And the Täj! The peerless Täj! What shall we

THE JESSAMINE BOWER IN THE PALACE AT AGRA.

say of its pure outlines, its perfect dome, its exquisite mosaic work in precious stones, its lace-like marble screens, its matchless symmetry!

> Thou didst gleam before our vision's eye,
> In dreams like fair mirage,
> And now before thy loveliness,
> Our lips are dumb, O! Täj.

It is indeed difficult to describe the Täj. Pictures can never do it justice, and, to crown all, it is in a garden so beautiful that the gem is enhanced by the setting. Above, in the palace, all is beauty, love and luxury; while in the resting-place of Shah Jahan and his adored wife, in this most beautiful tomb of the world, all speaks again of undying affection, peace and beauty.

But what of the dungeons underground? We had to insist on seeing them before the guide would escort us down. Then he opened the trap door and we descended. The heat seemed to grow more intense as we proceeded, while the flare of torches and their smoke reminded one of some of Dante's weird imaginings. Here, in the small underground rooms, the queens were imprisoned who incurred the king's displeasure. Here they were tortured or starved until it pleased him to set them free, or else taken to be hanged in the awful prison-room, directly under the Samam Burj, or Jessamine Tower. The beam above the pit is beautifully carved and, near by, is a little mosque wherein they uttered their last prayers. The pit opened out into the Jumna River, into which their bodies were

cast to be eaten by crocodiles. Here, too, is orientalism and false religion. The glamour is above, the awful dungeons below.

Lucknow, dating from 1775, was the capital of Oudh, which became a kingdom in 1814 under Ghazi-ud-din, the first king. It is chiefly of interest to tourists as being the scene of a siege in the awful days of the Mutiny of 1857. The old ruined residency, where Lawrence and his brave companions held out for those dreadful eighty-five days of siege, tells its own story of shot and shell, death and loss. As we walked through the underground room where three hundred women and children found shelter the whole awful scene came before our eyes. The little force intrenched, the thousands of rebels outside, the hourly death, the awful suspense until, on the 25th of September, Outram's forces came to the rescue. In Cawnpore there is a memorial erected over the well, wherein so many women and children, dead, dying and living, were thrown by the order of the murderous Nana Sahib, the leader of the mutineers.

In Lucknow we visited the grave of Sir Henry Lawrence, one of the noblest soldiers and Christians that ever lived. Tennyson has immortalized the siege in his fine poem by that name.

To-day the banner of England floats over Delhi's great fortifications and Ägra's equally impregnable fortress—impregnable to all but Anglo-Saxon bravery and daring. Here in Delhi and Ägra, symbols of Mogul magnifiecence; and in Lucknow, of ancient Oudh, we feel a thrill of pride for our race and join heartily

THE FORT AGRA—INSIDE THE FORTIFICATIONS ARE THE PALACE AND MOSQUE.

with our English brothers in giving honor to the great
and brave generals and men who won back all these
castles, forts, gardens and power for the English
crown.

Banner of England! O! not for a season hast thou
Floated in conquering battle or flapt to the battle-cry.
Never with mightier glory, than when we had reared thee
  on high,
Flying at the top of the roofs in the ghastly siege of Lucknow.
Shot through the staff or the halyard, but ever we raised thee
  anew,
And ever upon the topmost roof our banner of England blew.
                                                —*Tennyson.*

This part of India is expressive of the magnificence
we always connect with the Orient. In many other
places there are fine castles and beautiful buildings, but
in contrast to these is the prevailing poverty of the
millions of low-caste, the shut-in, ignorant condition
of the women, and all the sluggishness of Eastern life.
With all its marble palaces and grand towers we say
with the laureate:

> Better fifty years of Europe
> Than a cycle of Cathay.

In Baroda there are fine palaces belonging to the
Gaekwär, as the ruler is styled. These, however, are a
mixture of oriental and occidental architecture and
might easily be the residences of wealthy persons of
Western lands, with proclivities for travel and Eastern
magnificence.

The ceilings, frescoes, oil paintings, tapestry and
wood carvings are very rich and mostly in excellent
taste, while the porphyry and feldspar vases in the

entrance hall are truly splendid; but while the palace and grounds partake of so much Western culture and taste, yet the elephant-stables and the armories are entirely Eastern in prodigality and luxuriousness. The number of elephants is often ninety-nine, but never one hundred, as that is considered an unlucky number. At the time of our visit there were but nineteen, some of them noble creatures. There is a house near the stables containing the housings and trappings for these regal animals. The two howdahs meant for royalty are overlaid with gold, with gold-embroidered silk hangings bordered with rich fringes of gold. The other howdahs, for the Gaekwär's bodyguard, are similar, only done in silver. There are necklaces and anklets of pure gold for the huge animals. Another anklet was shown us, made of iron and ornamented (?) with sharp, needle-jointed spikes about a finger's length each, all pointing inward. These are used in catching the wild elephants. A tame decoy-elephant is sent into the jungle and, when the mahouts, or elephant-drivers, see the new elephants come up they shoot off firecrackers and guns to bewilder the poor animals. When there is a good deal of smoke, one of the most adroit manages to fasten one of these iron anklets around a leg of one of the wild creatures. This is fastened by a long, strong chain to a very large tree, and, after several days of fasting and struggle, the poor elephant gives up the battle and obeys its master.

In the other armory the trappings for the bullocks may be seen. These animals draw the ammunition-wagons and must present a fine appearance, in purple,

scarlet and gold. Even their horns are enclosed in hollow sheaths of gold. The climax of magnificence was supposed to be reached by the present Gaekwar's grandfather, who made two solid silver cannon, having iron bores. This man's son, however, outdid him by constructing two solid gold cannon to establish his name and fame.

In Mysore the palaces are somewhat like those in Baroda, partaking very largely of Western architecture and art. The summer home of the Rani is at Ooctacamund in the Nilgiri hills. It is quite modern in style and furnishings.

In Jeypore they are more oriental, but Delhi and Ägra contain the only fair samples of oriental magnificence and regal splendor. Here we may dream the Arabian Nights' dream over again—here revel in esthetic beauty and be filled with gratitude that we live in a more utilitarian age and may enjoy this ancient beauty and romance at a safe distance from the dungeons and the squalor that accompany despotism on the left hand, while fragrance, luxury and pomp step gaily on his right.

CHAPTER XV.

ABOUT CASTE.

The common belief among the Hindus as to the origin of the four great divisions of caste may be very briefly stated. The Brahmins proceeded from the mouth of Brahma; the Kshatriyas, or Chhatris, as sometimes spelled, from his arms; the Vaishays from his thighs, and the Sudras, or Shudras, from his feet. The extract quoted in support of this view I find in a condensed compilation in regard to caste prepared by Sir. J. Murdock. It is found in the ninetieth hymn of the tenth book, called "Purusha Sukta," or "Hymn to Purusha":

1. Purusha has a thousand heads, a thousand eyes, a thousand feet.

6. When the gods performed a sacrifice, with Purusha as the oblation, the Spring was its butter, the Summer its fuel and the Autumn its offering. This victim, Purusha, born in the beginning, they immolated on the sacrificial grass; with him the gods, the Sadhyas and the Rishis sacrificed.

11. When (the gods) Purusha, into how many parts did they cut him? What was his mouth? What arms (had he)? What (two objects) are said (to have been) his thighs and feet?

12. The Brahmin was the mouth; the Rajanya was made his arms; the being (called) the Vaishya, he was his thighs; the Sudra sprang from his feet.

13. The moon sprang from his soul, the sun from his eye, Indra and Agni from his mouth, and Vayu

from his breath. From his navel arose the air, from his head the sky, from his feet the earth, from his ear the four greatest.

In this manner (the gods) formed the worlds.

This hymn is, however, considered one of the latest of the Vedic hymns and (probably) belongs to the Brahmana period; hence it may have been written to suit existing orders or classes. Manu also gives a similar account of the origin of caste. In the "Mahabharata," one of the most voluminous of the Hindu books, a different account is given. Here it is stated that the world, being created by Brahma, the people were all Brahmins, but became separated by occupation and by high or low moral character into the four great castes. In another part of the same book the creation of caste is ascribed to Krishna. In still another "Purana" the "Krita age" is described as having only one caste. All this contradiction and confusion gave rise to one of the truest remarks in the "Mahabharata," which is: "Contradictory are the Vedas; contradictory are the Shastras; contradictory all the doctrines of the holy sages." Yet with all the inconsistency and even absurdity of these various accounts, Hindus believe firmly in the divine institution of caste.

Although scholars have proved without doubt that the European races and the Aryans have all come from the same place and at one time lived together as brothers, yet the Hindu still regards the European as an unclean *Mlechcha*. Outward honor is given all over India to the *sahib log* as the ruling race, but inwardly they throw contempt upon us. They despise

power, yet the Brahmin rules and sways India in a most tyrannical manner through the blighting caste system. Manu says the mixed castes, the almost endless subdivisions and resubdivisions, came into existence through marriages between the four original castes. But Max Müller thinks they originated in occupations and professions, trades, etc. It is this system which now holds sway in society. One of the possible good effects of such a system, Monier Williams points out, is the feasibility of governing such a people, since, being so widely separated by caste barriers, political fusion and therefore combined opposition are rendered very difficult.

Many other reasons for the subdivision of caste are given, as jealousy between rival families, clan-government, causing clans belonging to the same caste, and sectarian differences as to new gods, new rites and new dogmas. Many able writers have devoted years of study to this subject, and our only aim has been to give in brief some of the conclusions arrived at by such writers as Dr. John Muir; Dr. Wilson, of Bombay, who published two large volumes on this subject; Mr. Sherring, of Benares, who gave very detailed information as to caste and its workings in three quarto volumes, and Sir J. Murdock, who has compiled quotations from the sacred books of the Hindus and from eminent writers on this theme. To comprehend something of the complexity of this subject and the almost endless ramifications into which it leads, the following condensed table, which I have prepared

from the Census Report of 1898 for the Central Provinces alone, may be of some assistance:

CASTES IN THE CENTRAL PROVINCES.

DOMINENT OR MILITARY.

MAIN CLASS.   SUB-DIV.
1. Girasia ....
2. Giyar .... 5 Sub-divisions
3. Gat ....
4. Kondarazula ....
5. Maratha ....
6. Rajput ....25 Sub-divisions
7. Sikh ....

CULTIVATORS.
1. Agamudayan ....
2. Agharia ....
3. Alia ....
4. Are .... 1 Sub-division
5. Agawar ....
6. Balya ....
7. Banka ....
8. Bare ....
9. Bargah ....
10. Bishnoc ....
11. Bhoyar .... 2 Sub-divisions
12. Burman and Shan tribes.........
13. Chasa ....
14. Cherwa ....
15. Dangi .... 3 Sud-divisions
16. Deswalii .... 1 Sub-division
17. Dora ....
18. Ghogia ....
19. Gurdi ....
20. Kachhi .... 4 Sub-divisions
21. Kalanga ....
22. Kalaryi ....
23. Kamaria ....
24. Kamma ....

According to good authority, the main divisions of the four great castes are as follows:

Brahmin (Priestly caste) ....
Dubai, Pau, Gaur, Jhujatia, Sanoria, Kanauzia, Kaththia, Choba.

Kshatriya or Chhatri (Warrior caste)..
Rajput, Jat, Ghuhär, Thakur, Sikh, Lodhi, Raj Gond, Gujar and Kyast.

Vaishyas (Tradesmen & Artisans).
Bania, Parwar, Aggarwal, Ninu, Kirar, Sumar, Khattri, Baguam, Kutwar, Chivar, Mahra.

Sudra or Shudra (Laboring & Servant caste & lower craftsmen) ......
Kusta, Kurmi, Dhobi, Bharga, Lohar, Kumbhar, Ahir, Qual, Gadarya, Kangar, Sansiya, Gidhya, Nat, Bazigar, Chumar, Balahi, Kuch-bandia, Mang, Dher, Basor, Bhangi.

Some authorities put the last four outside the pale of caste altogether. In many parts of India the names would be quite different, just as in different parts of India the rules governing the same castes are very unlike.

Sir Monier Williams remarks that the lower castes are not unhappy, and, strange to say, none are greater sticklers for their caste observances. I am myself inclined far more to the opinion expressed by Raja Sir

T. Madhava Row, K. C. S. I., and quoted in Sir John Murdock's pamphlet:

> The longer one lives, observes and thinks, the more deeply does he feel that there is no community on the face of the earth which suffers less from political evils nor more from self-inflicted or self-accepted or self-created, and, therefore, avoidable evils, than the Hindu community

The second expression especially suits the condition in India—namely, self-accepted. They are born into these conditions and are taught the precepts and rules of their caste from infancy. Scarcely a famine waif, picked up and sheltered during the two famines of 1897 and 1900, even though the age was no more than four years, and though emaciated to a skeleton, but could on inquiry tell its jät (caste).

On all sides you see the observance of minute caste rules. A child strikes its foot against a stone and immediately makes an obeisance and salaam to the stone to propitiate the spirit possessing it. A man proceeds to go down a well, but not until he performs *puja* (worship) to the rope so that it may not break and precipitate him below. You offer some bread or food to a hungry child; he refuses, but implores you to give him money, as he can buy raw grain and prepare it himself, so it will not be contaminated by your touch. Your cordial hand-shake is refused by the zenana women for fear it may entail an extra bath of purification before they can prepare the next meal. Many castes dare not even receive a picture card from your hands. You must first lay it down, and then the other is free to lift it up and enjoy it. And so it goes through all the minutiæ of the daily duties.

At one time there was a severe struggle between the Brahmins on one side and the Buddhists and Jains on the other, the two latter being opposed to caste. When the Brahmins triumphed they made many laws stricter than before. Marriages permitted by Manu were forbidden, making it impossible for pure castes to intermarry with mixed castes, and the different subdivisions of the same castes were kept aloof from each other as if they were distinct castes. Mr. Sherring, of Benares, enumerates nearly two thousand subdivisions of Brahmins. They are engaged in all sorts of employments, from the haughty priests of Benares to the potato-growers of Orissa, who are described by Sir William Hunter as half-naked peasants with a filthy little Brahminical thread over their shoulders.

There are many defenders of caste in India. Very often some of the most energetic are educated men of the Hindu community. Some may and do deride the system; yet, as has been said, such a one may become a veritable Demosthenes in eloquence, only to sink into quiet submission to all the requirements of a superstitious family in private.

The advantages claimed for it are cleanliness, protection, division of labor, respect for authority and moral restraint. "Cleanliness" does not necessarily accompany ceremonial purity, as witness the use of cow's urine and dung as purifying agencies. "Protection" in sickness or distress, so far as it comes from caste-fellows, is a very unimportant consideration as observed in India. The *Panchayat* is very quick to

punish caste infringements, but exceedingly slow to extend the helping hand. A man may be sentenced to give an expensive dinner to his fellow-caste men (compulsory hospitality) for drinking from a low-caste man's cup or taking food from a European; but that same man may die in extreme want, with never a hand to aid him from among his own people. Should a Good Samaritan of a Christian doctor care for and feed him, he will be excommunicated for accepting this help. Should he recover he will be compelled to give a dinner to recover his caste. So great is the fear of ostracism that he may apply to the very Christian who helped him to give him the means of giving the dinner which is to purify him from the pollution caused by receiving food and care from his "unclean" benefactor. "Division of labor" is accomplished in other countries without the tyranny of such a system. "Respect for authority" in this case is degraded cringing to a power felt to be supreme, yet proceeding from one class of men—the Brahmins. "Moral restraint" means really "caste restraint," for things sinful in the sight of a holy God may be allowed and trivial things condemned as heinous caste crimes. During the Mutiny of 1857 Nana Sahib, at Cawnpore, sent cruel men to murder helpless English women and children and acted in the most shameful and treacherous manner toward those he had promised to protect. All this did not pollute him, but had he spared a little English girl and taken from her hands a drink of pure water he would at once have been expelled from caste.

Over against the supposed good results of caste we have, from the writers on Indian reform, both native gentlemen and great English authorities, the following evil effects attributed to caste: Physical degeneracy, owing to the narrowing circles wherein marriage is permitted, and also the laws enjoining infant-marriage. Intellectual ambition smothered. If all Hindu literature is considered part of religion, and the Brahmins alone estimated fit to read and teach it, intellectual stagnation must follow, not only in other castes, but to an alarming extent among the Brahmins themselves. When knowledge is insured in perpetuity to one class, it is no longer their interest to increase it, but rather to grow indolent and subsist by cheating and deluding the masses.

Thousands of Hindus would gladly help to institute social reforms, but caste ostracism has its terrors for even such enlightened men. Sir Monier Williams, in his book on "Brahminism and Hinduism," gives a striking account showing how caste is the foe of social reforms. He says:

When I was in Gujerat, in 1875, a man named Lalla-Bhai, a cloth merchant of Ahmedabad, was proved to have committed a heinous caste-crime. He had married a widow of his own caste, and to marry a widow is, in the eyes of a Hindu, a most awful offense. A woman once married belongs to one husband for time and eternity. Forthwith he was sentenced to complete excommunication. No one, either of his own, or any other caste, was to be allowed to associate with him; no one was to have any trade dealings with him; no one was to marry any of his children; no temple was to receive him as a worshiper; and if he died, no one was to carry his body to the burning-ground. On the morning after the sentence was passed he went to the Bazaar as usual,

but not a person would buy from him or sell to him; he could get no home to live in and none of his debtors would pay him their debts. It was impossible to sue them, as no one would give evidence. He was a ruined man, and had to leave the country, and obtain government employment in a distant city.

Nationality cannot exist in such a conflicting state of society. Sir J. Murdock describes caste conflicts in South India, where the hold of caste is said to be the strongest. These often occur elsewhere, and, when stopping short of contests, smouldering hatred and contempt are cherished. Hinduism and caste are inseparable; therefore all the evil results of class hatred, indifference to suffering and many other evils are fostered and consecrated by religion. Someone has said: "The spirit of caste will never die." We see something of it in other countries; but outside of India all reformers can appeal to religion as opposed to such enmity among brothers of the same human family. Here all the forces and precepts of religion are on the side of antagonism and oppression. Dreadful stories of neglect can be gathered from all parts of India. Travelers are left to die for want of water, because the jät or caste of the man is not known, and on the roads leading to sacred shrines many whitening bones testify to the cruelty of a system which so completely ignores the brotherhood of man.

Some maintain that the lower castes are not unhappy; some likewise deny that the *women* of India are unhappy. We see much to contradict both assertions in the caste conflicts before mentioned—the assumption of caste in South India by Dravidian, Turanian or Scythian peoples; the efforts of even many

Christian converts to retain rank of former caste, if high, and to claim as high a former caste as possible. "Manufactured Brahmins" in the north are cited by Hunter, and in South India Dr. Burnell says he knows families claiming to be Brahmins, and called so, who from inscriptions can be proved to have been Jains five hundred years ago. All these things prove that sorest discontent and even rebellion are rife. But even if content, their very content proves their degradation. How can men be content to be considered unclean and vile and in some castes ranked beneath even the brutes?

The Brahmin arrogates to himself even godlike powers. Witness the verse translated from the Sanskrit:

> The whole world is under the power of the gods;
> The gods are under the power of the *mantras;*
> The mantras are under the power of the Brahmin;
> The Brahmin is therefore our God.

With such ideas, how can justice prevail between man and man? All these evils are common throughout India, but probably the worst abuse comes to pass in the "Kulinism" of Bengal. A king named Ballala Sen, a reputed son of the Brahmaputra River, gave the title of *Kul*, or honorable, to certain Brahmins. Brahmins of a lower order are most anxious to get a Kulin son-in-law. Hence large sums are paid them to marry their daughters. There are Kulins with twenty, fifty, or even a hundred wives. But the marriage of Kulin females is cruelly stringent. These must not on any account be given to any unless they are of an equal or superior grade. The poor Kulin father is often in the

greatest difficulty. He cannot allow his daughter to marry anyone of a lower grade; he cannot afford to purchase a husband in his own. It would be a great disgrace to allow her to remain unmarried. His only resource is to appeal to some decrepit old Kulin Brahmin, who has already a multitude of wives, to save the honor of the girl and her family by adding one more wife to his lot. Kulin polygamy carries with it a license to indulge, to an almost unlimited extent, the vilest passions of human nature, carrying in its train untold misery, suffering and crime. It is, indeed, "hallowing wrong by the authority and sanction of religion."

It is pointed out in Sir J. Murdock's pamphlet on caste that even the British Government seems to sanction and abet caste distinctions by reporting in its census tables all the different divisions and subdivisions, which could safely be ignored; also by entering caste distinctions in other public documents and making inquiries in court about caste. Should government ignore this question, especially in giving posts of employment to applicants, and consider qualifications only, a great disintegrating factor would be introduced into the system.

To close with a few of the laws of many regarding caste will probably be the best commentary on this powerful system, which rules India with a rod of iron. These quotations, as well as the most of the material used in this chapter, are taken from Sir J. Murdock's compilation regarding caste. The works of Manu, said to have originally consisted of one thousand chapters

and one hundred thousand *slokas,* or proverbs, have been reduced to twelve thousand; these to four thousand, and then to two thousand, six hundred and eighty-five. A few quotations are given:

BRAHMINS.—THEIR CLAIMS.

92. Man is declared purer above the navel; therefore the purest (part) of him is said, by the Self-Existent, to be his mouth.

93. Since he sprang from the most excellent part, since he was the firstborn, and since he holds the Vedas, the Brahmin is, by right, the lord of all this creation.

94. His, the Self-Existent, after having performed penance, created in the beginning from his own mouth, for presentation of oblations to the gods and offerings to the manes (and) for the preservation of all this (world).

95. What being is there superior to him, by whose mouth the gods eat oblations and the manes offerings?

98. The birth of a Brahmin is a perpetual incarnation of *dharma,* for he exists for the sake of *dharma,* and is for the existence of the Vedas. (Dharma means religion or sanctity.)

99. When the Brahmin is born he is born above the world, the chief of all creatures, to guard the treasures of *dharma.*

100. Thus, whatever exists in the universe is all the property of the Brahmin; for the Brahmin is entitled to all by his superiority and eminence of birth.

101. The Brahmin eats his alone; wears his own and gives away his own; through the benevolence of the Brahmin, indeed, the other people enjoy (all they have). (Book I.)

PUNISHMENTS OF BRAHMINS.

379. Shaving the head is ordained as (equivalent of) capital punishment in the case of a Brahmin, but in the case of other castes, capital punishment may be (inflicted).

380. Certainly (the king) should not slay a Brahmin even if he be occupied in crime of every sort, but he should put him out of the realms in possession of all his property and uninjured (in body).

381. No greater wrong is found on earth than killing a Brahmin; therefore the king should not even mentally consider his death. (Book VIII.)
The atonement for killing a Sudra is the same as for killing the following animals:

132. On killing a cat, an ichneumon, a daw, or a frog, a dog, a lizard, an owl, or a crow, he should practice the observance (ordained for) killing a Sudra. (Book XI.)

SUDRAS.—CREATED FOR SERVITUDE.

91. One duty the Lord assigned to a Sudra—service to those (before mentioned) classes, without grudging. (Book XI.)

413. But a Sudra, whether bought or not bought, the Brahmin may compel to practice servitude; for that Sudra was created by the Self-Existent merely for the service of the Brahmin.

414. Even if freed by his master, the Sudra is not released from servitude; for this (servitude) is innate in him. Who then can take it from him?

410. The king should make the Sudra (act) as the slave of those who are twice-born. (Book VIII.)

123. Merely to serve the Brahmins is declared to be most excellent occupation of a Sudra; for if he does anything other than this, it profits him nothing.

129. Indeed, an accumulation of wealth should not be made by a Sudra even (if he is) able (to do so), for a Sudra getting possession of wealth merely ignores the Brahmin. (Book X.)

417. A Brahmin may take possession of the goods of a Sudra with perfect peace of mind, for, since nothing at all belongs to this Sudra, as his own, he is one whose property may be taken away by his master. (Book VIII.)

REWARD OF SERVITUDE.

125. The leavings of food should be given him and the old clothes; so, too, the blighted part of the grain; so, too, the old furniture.

PUNISHMENT OF SUDRAS.

270. If a man of low birth assault one of the twice-born castes with violent words, he ought to have his tongue cut out, for he is of the lowest origin.

Then, indeed, must India be populated with only "small souls," for any recognition of men as brothers outside the class or clan is a foreign doctrine.

At a large meeting in Calcutta fifty years ago the same sentiment by Burns was hailed with enthusiasm:

> For a' that and a' that
> It's comin' yet for a' that
> That man to man the world o'er,
> Shall brothers be for a' that.

And yet in fifty years what has been done inside of Hinduism to cure this evil? It will require something mightier than social reforms, mightier than human agency, to overcome and cast down this awful power of caste. Dr. Duff's words, quoted in Murdock's pamphlet, contain the key to the only solution:

> What, then, can exorcise this demon-spirit of caste? Nothing! Nothing but the mighty power of the Spirit of God, quickening, renewing and sanctifying the whole Hindu world! It is grace, not argument; regeneration of nature, not any improved policy of government — in a word, the GOSPEL, the everlasting Gospel, and that alone, savingly brought home by the energy of Jehovah's Spirit, that can effectually root out and destroy the gigantic evil! And it is the same energy, inworking through the same Gospel of grace and salvation, that can and will root out and destroy the other monster-evil under which India still groans —Idolatry and its grim satellite, superstition!

As caste and idolatry sprang up together from the same rank soil of old nature, both are destined to fall together. Then will the stupendous fabric of caste and idolatry be seen falling down like Dagou before the ark of the living God!

CHAPTER XVI.
PECULIARITIES AND INCONSISTENCIES OF CASTE.

When we speak of the "system" of caste a Western man conceives the idea of regular rules, divisions and customs. Upon the contrary, while its reign is an iron reign and millions bow to its tyranny, yet in itself it is one of the most contradictory and inconsistent systems imaginable. A missionary once told us that he wrote, while in college, an essay on "Caste in India," which was considered by all, himself included, as a very fair and comprehensive treatment of the subject. Now, after ten years' residence in India, working among all classes of people and hearing constantly of the bewildering rules and requirements of caste, he feels incompetent to give a settled opinion on this question, involving the accumulated ideas of centuries.

I have heard Brahmins flatly deny as their customs things which I have myself seen other Brahmins do, and we find in various parts of India similarly conflicting conditions and demands. Many of these differences come from the fact that not a few high castes here and there in India are manufactured ones—as, for instance, Rajputs, through prowess at arms, or through wealth, support their claim to be Brahmins. In South India many grand Telugu and Tamil families succeed in being classed and recognized as Brahmins, though not even belonging to the Aryan race, being

tions by speaking of the scrupulously clean zenanas. The bare interiors impress many people with the idea of cleanliness, but a closer inspection generally discovers the sanitary condition to be frightful. In most families the children are not even taught the habits considered essential in animal pets in our homes. There are exceptions to this rule, and in some few houses real cleanliness obtains and not merely ceremonial purity. But the prevalence of plague, the drastic cleansing measures adopted by government, the epidemics of typhoid, smallpox and other infectious diseases are sufficient testimony to the unclean conditions of streets, houses, wells and rivers. Just watch the bathers in a small river or tank, from which each one emerges purified (?), and you will be convinced. The whole body is being cleansed, coughings, spittings are going on—but I refrain—while the man three feet below is taking a morning drink of running, therefore pure (!), water! To hear of a man undergoing purification sounds clean, as does purifying (?) a well. But when we learn that the latter is plastered with cow manure to cleanse it, we gasp; and when we find the purification of the man consists in swallowing a pill composed of three products of the cow—milk, butter and the excretions—we feel that we cannot solve the question of Hindu purity. A high-caste man, rolling out his *chapatties* (bread cakes) will stop to blow his nose; having no handkerchief, he rubs his hand on his loin-cloth and proceeds with the rolling. The dexterous fingers in the zenana, making the delectable pän, will pause to pick something from the toes and

proceed with the pän without even a ceremonial washing. The sweetmeat man, in weighing out his goods, will spill them all over his bare feet and gather them up and add them to those on the scales without even an apology. As for the cloth covering the sweeties, it represents considerable wealth of butter and sugar accumulations. As to the habits of servants, every missionary can tell his tale of woe. Some of our friends at home would starve, I fear, if they tried to hold on to the ideas of cleanliness they have always cherished, or else do no mission work in order to look after their own health. This is one of the minor crosses in this land, though at times comedy leaves the stage and tragedy takes its place.

Mr. and Mrs. Kullman, no doubt, lost their lives the same day because of the unclean condition of a cooking vessel, while two other missionaries near Madras died from a similar cause. There are no doubt many such cases near us. Here in the Central Provinces three English officials died before morning after a dinner. The dishwater in which the plates were washed after each course was found to be deadly poison by reason of germs.

In the land where some castes are enjoined to bathe five, six and even thirty times a day we are in constant peril of losing our lives through uncleanliness. How many of us have sighed for a drink of *clean* water, not boiled, from a *clean* well, removed from drains, from a *clean* bucket in which hands have not been washed surreptitiously, from a *clean* cup which has been already wiped on a *clean* towel (not pre-

viously used for toilet purposes), and cleansed previously in *clean* water, in which lurk no germs of disease! Alas! for bathings oft and the purifications and ceremonies of caste! As the baseless fabric of a vision they fly away.

Kindness to animals! Perhaps in no one thing is the utter contradiction of precept and practice more apparent than in the reverence given to animals and the treatment they receive. Because the cow, the sacred bull, the peafowl, elephant, monkey and snake are worshiped in India, therefore it is concluded that here is the animals' paradise, and the poor dumb creatures of Western lands are commiserated on their hapless lot.

Jains are often seen going about the country wearing a thin cloth tied over nose and mouth so that they may not destroy animal life. These men will not wade a river for fear of crushing small creatures beneath their feet. Poor people, unable to feed Brahmins or beggars (I was going to say *other* beggars, for so many Brahmins fatten on free gifts from the poor), will go along the road with handfuls of crumbs feeding the ants under the trees or throwing the crumbs to the birds. This all sounds very pitiful and kind, yet in no other country is the lot of the brute creation such a hard one. Readers of English and American journals are often admonished of their duty to the dumb creatures about them because even heathen people are merciful to their animals. We are told again and again of that wonderful hospital for animals in Bombay. The only really pleasant thing about it,

the gateway, is photographed and reproduced in papers and magazines, until we fairly long to escort some of these enthusiastic Hinduites into the interior. Could they pay but one visit there we should never see its gateway portrayed in the magazines again. The maimed and miserable creatures within, without medicine or treatment, and, for the most part, underfed, make one's heart ache for pity. The cage of yelping, thin, mangy bazaar dogs, whose speedy death would be a mercy to themselves and a benefit to human beings who may be endangered if they escape, the wretched arrangements and revolting sights, are sufficient to convince anyone that only mawkish sentiment prompts the building and maintaining of such a hospital. At one time a roomful of bedbugs were cared for, poor men being hired by the night for eight cents to sleep there in order that the creatures might feast upon the miserable humanity. Outside the hospital are crowds of uncared for beggars, while within is this mockery of care for animals. The worship of the cow and sacred bull, though it may allow certain sleek animals, which have been blessed by the priests, to roam the grain bazaars and eat their fill from the stores of the poor grain-sellers, does not by any means insure good treatment to animals even of the bovine character. Such emaciated, scarred, ill-fed, ill-treated cattle you will never see anywhere else. As for hobbled horses, ponies and cows, space forbids the story. The little donkeys are nearly all lame from excessive burdens and scant food, while hundreds are beaten constantly on already sore and bleeding backs. The bazaars are

full of starving cats, dogs and goats, and many cruel things are done for gain or out of laziness which I think are unknown in Western lands. Once, when going up the ghat road to a hill station, we were unwise enough to take a cheap pony-carriage. The ponies nearly succumbed. Beatings were of no avail. We were growing weary of the brutality of the driver and also very anxious to get on, as we had no wish to spend the night on the road, for tigers were not entire strangers there. "Oh, we'll soon make them go," the driver said, as we neared some huts. One of the men ran into one of these huts and returned with something in his hand. We supposed that he had a little grain for the poor, jaded beasts. When he went to the ponies' heads something aroused our suspicions, and my husband jumped out in time to see the man trying to rub red pepper into the eyes of the exhausted creatures. Our merciful intervention was the cause of our camping under a tree in the rain for a couple of hours until more ponies could be secured.

The absurdity of worshiping the sacred bull and its small indication of gentleness to animals, even of the same kind, may be illustrated by a little scene I witnessed at a Hindu festival. A beautiful, sleek, well-fed young bullock was mounted on a cart and being drawn around the fair to receive the salutations of the people and their offerings of grain, grass, sugar and salt. The handsome young animal looked happy and well cared for. But what of the poor bullock drawing the cart? Thin, hungry, goaded on by sticks in which nails were fastened, causing its poor sides to

bleed afresh with each thrust! And this in a land where animals are worshiped!

A lady in an American paper suggested that, as the Hindus loved animals so much and held their life so sacred, it would be easy to organize bands of mercy and help among them. Mercy and help—ah! How both are needed in a land where children are purposely crippled in order to beg more successfully for lazy parents and guardians! In South India even such a horrible practice is known as fastening beetles on children's eyes to eat them out. Can there be mercy and help among high castes where baby-widows are treated worse than criminals would deserve? But at any rate, some will say, the taking of life is avoided. What life? Caste forbids the killing of a cow or a chicken; therefore an only son in a Brahmin family is left to die sooner than give him the beef or chicken broth which the doctor, himself a Hindu, said would in all probability save his life. At the same time this family's caste does not forbid the eating of fish. Save the life of a broken-legged horse, but ride another with bleeding back an unmerciful distance! There is no soundness in the Hindu creed of the sacredness of life. It is an illogical, blind following of caste rules which ameliorates the condition of neither animal nor man.

Among the people who observe the purdah or gosha system we find, amid all its hardships and privations, many seeming and real breaches of its letter and spirit. In many very high families the old mother or grandmother will sometimes appear and talk before

men, but the younger women are supposed never to
be seen by other than relatives. What was our surprise, then, while calling upon a family of rank, to
have a young and beautifully adorned bride brought
in and shown to my husband! And that, too, in presence of her own husband and another male relative!

In many houses where we teach, should the husband appear, the wife will fly from our presence, leaving us to face him alone, thus demonstrating her own
superiority over the foreign ladies. Even the oil-man
or water-carrier must give notice of his approach, so
that the women may hide behind pillars or doors. Yet
in these same families, if a man comes on business, one
of the women will often talk to him from behind a
door or pillar, and in a lull of the conversation, pre-
tending to think he is gone, she will look out, showing
her face entirely; then, with a little scream, disappear
again. From a young European woman who has
worked for years in the zenanas I learn that much flir-
tation and even real sin is possible behind the purdah.
There is, after all, only one effectual purdah, and it is
the gospel one: "Blessed are the pure in heart."

There are some strange practices connected with
the naming of children. We all know how the Brahmins despise the Bhangis, or Mehtars, and to tell one
of them that he acts like a Mehtar is the grossest insult. Yet these proud people will give these very
names to their children in the hope that the children
may thus be rendered displeasing to the gods, and
that, in consequence, the gods will not desire to take
them. Similar to this is the Western superstition, that

if you love your child too much God will take it from you. In a Brahmin family which I know five children died in succession, each soon after its birth. When a sixth came, and that a fine-looking boy, they quickly gave it the name Bhangi (pronounced Bungi). After two years more a little girl was born, and they called her Mehtrani. Both names mean scavenger. As these two children lived, it would be difficult to dislodge the superstition which has fastened such opprobrious epithets on their children. Another family who would dislike very much to be considered Christians, nevertheless named a child, born during the famine, when the family were receiving help from the mission, Isa Charan—"At the feet of Jesus."

Some of the most inconsistent features of caste relate to food. In certain Banyia castes a man may not eat food prepared in any home but his own, or by anyone outside his own family, with one notable exception. He may eat it, prepared away from home and by others than relatives, provided it is prepared in ghee. Now, the reason for this is that, as feasts in connection with marriages are necessary parts of the ceremonies, and as those attending the weddings must be able to eat there, the enactment that food prepared with ghee may be eaten away from home assures the expensiveness of the food.

These same Banyias may not sell honey or beeswax, as they are products manipulated by the mouth of the bee. Other less particular castes may sell these contaminated articles. You may cause great loss to a sweetmeat seller by touching the sweets on his plate

or tray, as you thereby spoil the whole stock. We did
this once, and, after tasting, decided not to buy, as the
wares were not fresh. "Give it to your dog, then. I
cannot sell it. You have touched it," the man said.
Yet these men make some of their finest goods with
sugar which they know has been clarified with bone-
dust, while another large part is made from *gurh,* or
unrefined cane-sugar, which one would think would be
sufficient to condemn it for high-castes. This *gurh*
is prepared by many castes, principally by Kachi,
Kurmi and Laria Chumär castes, which are all composed of Sudras. In no other particular can they
come near the lofty Brahmin, who would throw away
any food that a Sudra had touched.

Now for a few hog stories, which show, perhaps,
the ridiculous side of caste rules and exceptions more
vividly than anything else. A hunter brought to the
bungalow five beautiful little white pigs. I was tempted
to buy them, being tired of goat meat, when the servants prepared to flee the compound in a body—high,
low, Hindu and Mohammedan, from the cook to the
water-carrier. I did not buy them; yet these same
servants will cook English salt pork, sausages, etc.,
and carry it in parcels from the railway station,
knowing exactly what they are doing. An amusing
thing occurred in South India in a mission-compound.
A wild-looking hog rushed on the premises from the
direction of the jungle. The servants declared it to be
a wild hog, and the missionary shot it. Two Brahmins
heard of the shooting and came in haste to get some
bristles to wear as charms. They tied some around

their necks, feeling well secured thereby against evil spirits. Alas! for their joy! The next day it was proved beyond question that the hog was a domestic animal owned by a Basor. It was being driven with others, and breaking away fled to the jungle. Marks on the animal identified it and confusion reigned. The two Brahmins were distracted over their errors. The *Panchaiyat* held its session on the spot, only far enough away to escape defilement, and the two unfortunate men were sentenced to give an expensive khana to their caste people on penalty of being excluded from caste if they refused.

Here is a still more astonishing story: On the sacred Narbudda River, at a place called Burman, you may see lordly Brahmins crawling prostrate under a stone image of a hog. If you are good, yet stout, the hog will raise itself to let you through; but if you are thin and bad, he will squeeze you down until you will be glad to draw back.

In the Vedas the *Viraha,* or boar-incarnation, is fully described. The story, by the way, is the Hindu version of the deluge; from whence derived, who can tell? A demon cast the earth into the sea and destroyed its population. Vishnu assumed the form of a huge boar, and with his powerful tusks raised the earth from the waters. This incarnation is usually spoken of as the *Barha* incarnation.

Just at the close of the *Dawali,* this year, a huge bazaar was held in front of the house of a man, Bhika by name. He was born a Basor, but became a sweeper by marriage and occupation. This man hires musicians

to attract the crowds and the market-people bring their goods there to sell. At this time he has a great sacrifice also. A booth is erected near his house, and in it an image of mud is made. This is called a *murlee,* and a mock marriage is often celebrated between this image and men attending the fair. At night a great sacrifice is made. A hog is slaughtered and offered to the idol. I could not find out the meaning of all this ceremony, even from the people themselves. They know very little of the inner meaning of such rites, and what they do know they hesitate to tell us. But what I wish to emphasize is the fact that in the evening all classes, from Brahmins down, come into this low quarter of the town, in front of a sweeper's house, and worship before an image which he has paid for and set up. All classes of Brahmins come, not only the Chattisgarhi Brahmins, as a Christian claiming descent from Brahmins suggested, but North India Brahmins and proud Marathas, even to a first-class magistrate.

How unfounded seems the hatred to beef and beef-eaters, as the Hindus call Europeans, when in their own books (the Vishnu Puranas) Monier Williams finds the fact stated that meat-eating was once universal in India, and the cow was sacrificed at certain festivals, when the aroma of the beef was considered as an excellent aliment for the spirits of the dead. Manu also, the great law-giver, sanctions the eating of all animal food, only stipulating that portions be offered to the gods and to spirits of ancestors. How absurd seems a sentence passed on a king of Travancore, who

was troubled on account of the lives he had destroyed in battle, that these sins would all be forgiven him if he should pass through the body of a cow! Fully as absurd was the manner in which he fulfilled the condition. A huge golden cow was made, and, after lying in its interior for three days, the king crawled forth absolved.

During famine times caste-rules undergo great strains. Some *Panchaiyats* passed special dispensations allowing caste people to eat at government poorhouses without losing caste, and many other subterfuges were resorted to. In most cases the people were true to caste and many doubtless died sooner than break its regulations.

In Gadawara, a few years ago, a man lost his wife and child in a burning house because he was not near enough to give them permission to leave it. They resisted all efforts made to remove them until it was too late. From a foolish notion of reverencing the master of the house they doubly bereaved him. Time fails to recount many other peculiar and contradictory things pertaining to caste—such as the workmen on the Darjeeling railway receiving caste sanction for meat-eating while on that difficult work. The strangest feature of it all is that the people themselves seem utterly blind to these absurdities. They bow unquestioningly to the dictates of this system and never inquire: Is it right? Is it consistent? or, Is it true? They simply bow. Well may we say, with Erasmus, of it and them, "So hard pressed are they by the

heavy yoke of man that they cannot take upon them the easy yoke of Christ."

But its sway shall not be forever. Here and there souls are awakening to a sense of caste-bondage and, realizing that "life is more than meat, and the body than raiment," are searching for the true rule of life which teaches that "not that which enters into a man defileth him, but that which proceedeth from the heart." A Hindu reformer cuttingly says, "Our religion seems to have its root in our stomachs," but by and by the new and purer doctrine will be believed throughout India, and instead of innumerable pharisaic injunctions as to food, cup and platter, the motto for Hindustan, as for the world, shall be: "Blessed are the pure in heart."

CHAPTER XVII.

EDUCATION IN INDIA.

Americans usually think of the people of India in a bulk, and call them "natives," making no distinction among them as to education, refinement or wealth. The word "native" suggests people like the wild tribes of Africa; hence many, through ignorance, put the people of India on a par with those tribes. Just why a man of India should be called a "native" rather than that a man born in Germany or France should be called a "native" when in his own country, may not be easy of explanation. Think of the shock to a Londoner in Regent Park if he were referred to as a *native.* Some one's head would be in danger.

An Indian lady recently perpetrated a good joke. She was intelligent, educated, refined and quite comely. She was lecturing in England on behalf of the Anti-Opium cause, and everywhere heard her own people spoken of as "natives" of India. An English lady said to her one day:

"Why do you return to India? You are good-looking, intelligent and attractive. You could marry an Englishman and live here."

"Oh, I wouldn't like to marry a *native,*" was her sarcastic reply, meaning a native of England, of course.

There are some wild people in India—a few, not

About that time William Carey, a Baptist missionary, appeared on the scene. To him more than to any other man is due the credit of founding education in India. Before his time some Lutheran missionaries had done something in the way of reducing a few vernaculars to writing and establishing schools. But Carey mastered the Sanscrit and a few of the vernaculars. His great thought was to get a literature. He established a printing-press, cast his own type in the vernaculars and began printing the Bible in the language of the common people. Marshman and Ward joined with Carey. After some years they had printed the Bible in twenty-six languages of India. Along with the Bible they printed school text-books, that the people might learn to read. Soon schools were established, especially by various missions, as these text-books made schools possible.

The introduction of these text-books into the vernaculars was the real beginning of general education in India. In the beginning there was great opposition to promiscuous education. The Brahmins foresaw their loss of prestige if the common people had access to books, and they strenuously opposed this innovation. Even within the past twenty years, when an Indian gentleman translated the Rig Veda into Bengali, there was great commotion among the Brahmins on account of the degradation of the sacred book by putting it into the hands of the common people.

The people of India are very conservative and reverence ancient customs. They are slow to take hold of anything new. They say, "My father and my grandfather could not read. I can't read. We have

prospered fairly well. Why should I have my son taught?" They had a sort of suspicion too that, as printing and books were introduced by the English, especially missionaries, they must be in some way connected with Christianity; that their sons in learning to read might be led away from the ancient faith.

It was not until within the past twenty-five years that the Indian youth manifested much desire for education. The most potent factor in producing this desire was the opening of a large number of government and railway offices to qualified Indian men. The Hindu, like other men, believes in a thing when he sees money in it, and when he saw good salaries and respectable employment offered him, his ambition began to awaken. But an education was required to fit him for these positions, and he began to call for schools.

The missionaries have done much in educating the Indian youth. Not only Carey and Marshman and Ward, but almost all missionaries, have turned their attention to this line. They have reduced nearly all the vernaculars to written languages; they have translated the Bible, school text-books and other useful books; they have provided schools for their converts and also for non-Christians, and urged the youth to attend and develop their minds for useful service. To-day a very large share of the schools and colleges of India are supported and managed by missionary organizations. They are doing a grand work also in industrial institutions and in orphanages. They have established training-schools for the teaching of trades, as weaving, cabinet-making, woodcarving, shoemaking,

lacemaking and like trades. The Reid Christian College of Lucknow is doing a grand work in teaching stenography and typewriting, and thus opening up a large field of usefulness.

Government is developing a thorough system of education in all the provinces and presidencies. It has five universities located at Bombay, Calcutta, Madras, Allahabad and Lahore. These five universities alone have power to grant degrees, as A. B., A. M., etc. Each has annual examinations in several centers within its own territory and within easy access to all the population. Pupils from the various schools are sent to the nearest examining center for examination for entrance to the university, or for A. B., A. M., M. D., LL.B., and other degrees. There are several commendable points in this system. Everyone in any part of India has about the same grade of examination for the degree he receives as every other one in any other province. This same plan applies to European as well as to Indian pupils.

It may be thought difficult for a student to pass the whole of his course at one examination. There are some mitigating elements, however. For example, the candidate for A. B. may take an examination at the end of his second year of college and receive his F. A. (First Arts); then, at the final examination, he has but two years' work upon which to pass. Then, also, the percentage of marks that will pass him is only about thirty, while in an American college it is seventy-five to ninety per cent.

CHRISTIAN GIRLS' SCHOOL, JUBBULPORE.

Government has primary schools in most of the towns and large villages. These are partly under the control of government and partly controlled by local committees of leading citizens of the community in which the school is located. The support of these schools comes from three sources—government funds, local funds and fees from pupils. The local committee decides how much each pupil shall pay, according to the ability of his parents or guardians. But these fees are very low, in some cases not over two cents a month.

There is, also, in many places, a sort of compulsory system. The local committee decides what pupils shall be compelled to attend school, or whose parents or guardians are so situated that they do not need the labor of their boys to support the family. Others may go if they choose.

In many places similar schools are provided for girls also. But these are not so general. Government offers special inducements to girls' schools, but as yet few Indian men think it necessary to have their girls taught. Many are so benighted still as to think that if women learn to read and write it unfits them for the house duties. It may unfit them to be the slaves of their husbands, but it does not unfit them to be companions and intelligent mothers.

Besides the primary schools, government has, in large centers, middle-schools, high-schools and here and there a college. Light fees are charged in these institutions also, as well as in the primary schools.

In each province and presidency there is an in-

spector-general of education, sometimes called by another name, but having the same functions. He has general charge of the educational interests of his province. There is a deputy inspector for each district or county. The deputy inspectors travel about their districts, examine the schools at least once a year, and report to their superior officers. They have the immediate oversight of the teachers, and report any delinquencies. Besides these there are usually circle inspectors, who grade between the inspector-general and the deputy inspector. Each of these circle inspectors has a group of districts under his charge. He has the oversight of the deputy inspectors and travels about inspecting the schools in his circle, and reports to the inspector-general. The inspector-general provides a curriculum for the schools of his province.

As previously intimated, there are many private and mission schools. These may be independent, if they like, but usually the managers place them under government inspection and receive from government an annual "grant-in-aid." The managers employ the teachers, furnish the building and apparatus and are responsible for the institution. They follow the government course of study and the deputy inspector examines the school at least once a year, promotes to the next grade the pupils that pass, and recommends to the inspector-general the amount of grant-in-aid to be given, which is based on the daily attendance and the number of passes. The grant-in-aid is never a very considerable sum, but is a great encouragement to pri-

vate institutions. These schools may teach whatever else they wish, but the government course must be pursued if they receive the grant-in-aid.

Most missions have orphanages in various places. These orphanages have become much more numerous in the recent famines. Many thousands of orphans are being educated, and, along with their school-work, they are usually taught some useful trade. Government also has industrial, technical and professional schools. Schools of medicine, law, engineering, forestry and surveying are established in various parts of India.

As yet only a very small percentage of the youth avails itself of the higher education. The primary schools are being urged upon the people. Most parents are now proud of their boys that can read and write, though few appreciate the value of such knowledge.

A serious problem presents itself in regard to college graduates. The college is a new institution. Graduates are a new class. As before mentioned, the primary object of the government officers in establishing schools for Indian youth was to prepare a certain number for government service. Now the supply is greater than the demand. A very few lines of employment are as yet open for these college graduates. Government service, railway service, teaching, clerkships with business firms, law and medicine are about the only objects of a graduate's ambition, unless he is a Christian and looks to the ministry. The legal profession is greatly overrun. As to medicine, its practice is not very general in India. The vast majority

O Bahar" is considered the finest production. Yet it is mostly twaddle. The plan of the story shows little or no genius. Its inspiration is derived from the coarsest passions. Gluttony is very prominent. Parts of it are so immoral that even the Munshis, when teaching the English people the language, ask them to omit a number of pages. Such literature is not fit to be placed before the student.

Again, the vernaculars are not rich enough in vocabulary and forms of thought to be used in higher education. A language is a growth; that growth is in proportion to the intellectual growth of the people using it. A pastoral people will develop a language rich in terms pertaining to the flocks and fields and tents; but they may have no words to express thoughts pertaining to the city. They may have no words to express the idea of a paved street, telephone, electric light, elevator, mayor, high-school, and the like, because these pastoral people have no such things and have never made words to express them. On the same principle these same vernaculars of India have no words to properly express evolution, chemical affinity, dynamics, telegraphy, corpuscles, perception and similar thoughts so common in modern science. But the English language is very fertile in words and phrases that will clearly represent all our thoughts on modern science and philosophy. Rather, therefore, than build up all the vernaculars to the standard of modern thought, it is much better to use the already prepared English language in all forms of higher education. The primary schools are in the vernacu-

lars of the people, but above the middle grade government has wisely decided to use English.

English is destined to become the language of the common people of India as well as of the educated. The people are anxious to learn it. As the rulers of the land are English, the people think that they are of more importance themselves when they can use the English language, and this is true. An Indian, as a rule, is more honored by his own people when he is able to speak English. He stands a better chance for employment, not only in government service, but in the service of Indian merchants and business men. The knowledge of English also opens to the Indian youth all the treasures of knowledge of the earth. Science, philosophy, art, poetry, inspiration are his. His mind necessarily expands and becomes better fitted for responsible service.

For the English language to become universal in India will not be very difficult. The Indian acquires a new language readily. Often a common cook may be found who speaks fluently four or five languages, English included. The desire to learn English is greatly increasing. Let the vernaculars pass away. They have little in them that need be preserved. The Sanscrit is already a dead language. It may be preserved as such, just as classic Greek or Hebrew is with us. One language for all India would be a great blessing.

The people of India are very distinct one from another. They will never become one nation until they have a common language. The common government (English) does a great deal even now to

make their interests one. Yet they remain as separate peoples. In the United States of America there are colonies of Russians, of Germans, of Bohemians, who retain the languages of their mother-countries. These never become Americanized as long as they retain their native languages. They do not come into perfect sympathy with the government or people of the United States in general, until they use the language of the United States as their daily language.

When the people of India use one tongue in all parts of the land, and have one government, their interests will be one and they will become one nation.

CHAPTER XVIII.

GODS AND RELIGIONS OF THE LAND.

The gods and goddesses in the Hindu Pantheon are almost innumerable. There are said to be thirty-three crores, or three hundred and thirty millions of greater and lesser deities. In fact, the religion of the Hindus has degenerated into a huge system of demonology. The woods, the fields, the trees and rivers are all inhabited by beneficent or malevolent spirits. Even animals are possessed by spiritual beings, good or bad.

This great host of gods would seem to give wide range of choice to worshipers, but choice, like caste, occupation and many other things in India, has been decided by a man's forefathers, centuries before he came into the world. If his ancestors were Saivites, or worshipers of Siva, he will be so likewise, else be accused of the deadly sin of changing his religion. The same is true of followers of Vishnu. Yet, in a way, Brahminism is broad—that is, it absorbs into itself many beliefs and practices, and a man may be a good Hindu and even believe in the Christ of the Bible, provided he does not contradict or denounce anything in Hinduism. He must believe *all* to be true, and above everything else, with his belief, he must keep caste.

While most of the numerous gods are worshiped in all parts of India, yet some have a decided pre-eminence in certain portions. The two superior gods are undoubtedly Siva and Vishnu. The great Hindu triad represented in a number of cave temples, notably in the colossal sculpture in the Elephanta* Caves, near Bombay, represents Brahma, the creator, in the center; Vishnu, the preserver, on the right; Siva, the destroyer and reconstructor, on the left. The creator, however, has been largely lost sight of, and the other two of the triad claim the homage of the millions.

Siva, in the central and northwestern parts of India, has hosts of followers. The revolting symbol of Maha-deo, as Siva is called, is seen everywhere— by the road side, in front of temples, and even in the houses of his worshipers. This symbol, the *Ling,* or *Linga,* is thought by some scholars to be mystical in meaning and to hold none of the sensual idea; but to one who has lived in India for a long time and become intimate with some of the ruling ideas, the worship of the *Yoni* and *Linga* explains much of the impurity of life prevailing in the land of Maha-deo.

In the whole valley of the Ganges this worship prevails, as the Ganges itself is supposed to flow from Siva's body as excretory matter. The Vishnuites, or Vaishnumites, as they are called, not to be outdone, try to attribute the source of the mighty Ganges to their god, and say it flows from his feet. Many quite as incredible and ridiculous stories are told of

---

*The Elephanta cave temple was excavated twelve centuries ago. It is now visited by thousands of tourists.

these and other gods and goddesses. Vishnu is worshiped mostly in his incarnated forms of Krishna and
Rama, but he himself has a distinct personality as
preserver and has hosts of devotees and a thousand
names and epithets. In many cases their temples
stand side by side, as at Kanjivaram, near Madras.
These two principal gods are Brahminical deities and,
according to most scholars, believed to be derived from
the Vedas, although some attribute to them a pre-
Aryan or non-Aryan origin.

Five principal divisions of Hinduism are usually
given, but they could all be considered under the two
great sects of Saivism and Vaishnavism. The five
given are (1) worshipers of Siva (Saivas), (2) worshipers of Vishnu (Vaishnavas), (3) worshipers of
female deities, such as the numerous wives of Siva
and wives of other gods (Säktas), (4) worshipers of
Ganesha, the elephant-headed god of luck and good
fortune (Gana-patyas), (5) sun-worshipers (Sauras).
A sixth is sometimes given—Pasupata or Kapalika,
which is chiefly found in South India.

The contemplative Hindu, studying the forces of
nature, noticed creation, preservation, destruction and
then reconstruction. He conceived of an eternal
essence, or the "Absolute," manifesting itself in these
processes; thus it became divided into many personali-
ties. The sun, showering blessings upon the earth,
became an object of worship. The productive
earth shared in the homage and, in like manner, whatever gave benefit was deified; so that the cow, the
fruitful womb, the running streams, a man's imple-
ments in agriculture and the arts—all in turn became

either deities or manifestations of them. In this way religion, while recognizing a first cause, in practice became pantheistic. The gods were endowed with the known attributes of human beings, and, being gods, these attributes were magnified. In turn the worship of these beings emphasized the same traits in the worshipers. So, in his search after God, and having no revelation of real purity, or having departed from that of his ancestors, the Hindu has fled from himself to a man-made god, and, copying its exaggerated traits, has grown no nearer righteousness, but has sunk and is sinking, supported only by borrowed ideas of holiness taken from the religions founded on revelation. At the close of this chapter more of the *results* of this system on individual and national life will be noticed.

All the gods are not worshiped alike in all parts of India. Each one holds sway in certain localities and among certain classes and sects, although many people worship a large number. The whole religion of ninety percent of the people of India is one of fear only. The elevation attained by a nation which worships what is pure and holy is lacking; for, though good spirits are believed to exist, yet they receive very little attention, because, if good, they will do no harm, therefore they need not be worshiped, while the bad must be propitiated lest they wreak vengeance upon the neglectful.

Ganesha and Su-brahmanya are favorite tutelary gods and they are asked for positive blessings, while Ayenar, a very popular god in South India, and but little known elsewhere, is only invoked to ward off

danger or disease. He is supposed to hold sway over demons and fiends who lie in wait to devastate fields and blight cattle. Offerings of the blood of goats, swine, sheep, cocks and other animals are made to him and also eatables. His priests are very poor and are said to be of the lowest caste. This latter statement is quite probable, considering the manifold inconsistencies of which Hinduism is capable. Ayenar and his two wives ride on horses over the fields, chasing away demons and spirits. This god is credited with a horrible origin, as the son of Siva and Vishnu, when Vishnu took the form of a beautiful woman. In Calcutta, Kali, the goddess who delights in the blood of goats and buffaloes, is a favorite deity, and a more loathsome creature than she is represented it were difficult to imagine. As Durga, this same goddess slew a demon by that name, and the festival in her honor in Bengal is greatly honored. In another form, Parwati, she is the popular god at Poona, where she is called the goddess of fortune. At Madura, in South India, she has many followers. In front of her shrine there living parrots and cockatoos are hung in cages.

Krishna is a favorite god in many parts of India, but his followers are generally very immoral. This is not to be wondered at, when the impure life attributed to the god is remembered. The very formula used in his worship, *"Radha Krishna,"* tells this story, for Radha was the wife of a cowherd and Lakshmi the lawful wife of Krishna; also his silly and immoral antics with the *gopis,* or milkmaids. About one-sixth of the natives of Bengal are his followers. Hanuman is a tutelary god in the Decca and in Central and

Northern India. At one time Ravana carried away Rama's beautiful wife, Sita, to Ceylon, from whence she was rescued by Hanuman. This caused his deification. This exploit is celebrated in the Hindu poem Ramayana. He was probably a real aboriginal chief, resembling an ape, and for his prowess in battle became celebrated. The tales about him came to be legends and were finally embodied in the poem mentioned. His image is generally very rough and smeared with red paint and the offerings are largely fine oil. As some claim him to be one of Siva's numerous sons, the symbol *Linga* is often seen in his temples. These symbols are constantly met with and there are at least thirty million of them in India. In Poona I saw a large image of this god under a banyan tree. In Benares there are not only images and temples, but real monkeys are sheltered and worshiped in many temples. These poor, disgusting, impudent creatures are fed by devotees.

To anyone believing in the philosophical beauty of Hinduism, one visit to sacred Benares is quite sufficient to disillusionize his mind. And so of Hinduism in general, for while mystical meanings may be attached by Pundits to many practices, as they are to the symbol of Siva, already mentioned, yet in its practical results among a people "wholly given over to idolatry" there is only corruption and decay. The few beautiful texts found in the sacred Veda are not generally known, and even in the Vedas themselves are only as grains of gold dust in heaps of débris. A few, an almost infinitesimal few, by austerities and prayers are really

seeking freedom from sin; but the masses of both high and low do not realize the disintegrating and decaying action of sin on the soul. Most are trying to propitiate the evil spirits or bribe the better ones to grant temporal blessings. While in theory professing to believe all desire is sin, even the desire for food, or for knowledge, yet in practice they are scheming for the least vestige of gain. With nothing before him but eight million or more of re-births, is it to be wondered at that the Hindu is despondent and unambitious, yet grasping? What but moral decay prompts infant marriages? Are they not born of the thought that profligacy is rampant and a virgin wife only possible when secured as an infant? Caste, too, is the legitimate outcome of a religion which is powerless to transform the life. Having no restraining power like that of a spiritual religion, and no teaching as to the brotherhood of man and the fatherhood of God, their conduct is regulated by the iron rule of caste, attention being paid to minor details while the weightier matter of morals has been neglected. All must admit that caste, in some particulars, has been a restraint; but the restraint relates chiefly to eating food, eating with other castes, marriage and occupation, while real morals are ignored. Whatever obedience a man pays to caste rules, or whatever almsgiving or feeding of animals he may perform, he counts as so much accumulated merit and, through and through the Hindu religion or religions the principle of self-righteousness is apparent. A man works out his own salvation. There is no power recognized that can cleanse from sin; no great, inspiring life to

move as an example among men. Krishna is sometimes likened to Christ, but his immoral life can have
no elevating influence whatever on his devotees. Even
the religious devotees who devote their entire time to
austerities and devotions are anything but the sort of
men to help any people to righteousness or honor.
These men are called fakirs, or *sadhus,* and are taught
by religion to mortify the flesh. This is done by disfiguring their bodies and living in nakedness and filth,
counting this uncleanness of body cleanness of soul.
Their hair remains uncut and uncombed, and often
their bodies are smeared with ashes of cow-manure,
while streaks of paint add to the hideous appearance.

They wander from place to place and are greatly
reverenced by the people, who accede to their demands
for gifts, and consider them a class of holy men. Even
proud Brahmins bow down to these grimy creatures.
Self-torture of every description is inflicted on their
bodies. Some hold their hands or feet in one position
until fixed there and impossible to be moved. Others
fasten their eyes upon a certain object for days or
months. A still more silly performance is to move
one finger up and down continuously during waking
hours. Many of these men measure the ground with
their bodies until they reach the sacred Benares; but,
no doubt, when arrived there they join the evil throng
which crowds the temples and shares in the religious
(?) revels sanctioned there. There is evil in every
land, but it is not connected with worship in any but
idolatrous countries. The pride of the Romans did
not keep the evils of sensuality even from the temples
of the vestal (?) virgins; nor did the Egyptians fail

to fall into religious uncleanness in the majestic temples of Isis. Exquisite Greece, in the midst of her refined, alluring and ornate gods and goddesses and glorious temples, crowning the marvelous Acropolis, fell into softness, effeminacy and final decay. No amount of culture, beauty and magnificence can preserve a nation or an individual who once loses the perfect ideal, the really divine, the vital touch of God. Then what of dark India, where every so-called divinity is more or less a villain and the semblances worshiped are themselves shapes of deformity, and where only the ancient temples, with their splendid carvings, seem to furnish any adequate background for the old mysticism of the Vedas? There the imaginary Mahatmas, inhabiting the snows of the Himalayas, and the wonder-working Sadhus, all vanish, and in their places one sees gross materialism of a sort unknown elsewhere. Where will you find the religious sanction of greed, bribery, theft and licentiousness, but in the shadow of the temples of Siva and Vishnu? Where, as in Brindaban, will you find six thousand temple-prostitutes? Where a little building, like the one at Pandrapur, which my husband saw, for the purpose of receiving illegitimate children, who are the result of the orgies practiced at this place in connection with the great religious festivals held there?

At the great *melas,* or festivals, held at various places besides those mentioned—Burman on the Narbudda, at Benares, Puri, Jagan-nath and elsewhere—there are many objectionable and disgusting practices and ceremonies, as noticed in other chapters. The

whole tendency is toward grossness and vulgarity. The very songs about the gods are obscene. The great attraction at many of these places is the *Jatra*, or religious drama. This, too, can only be bad in influence, as the characters represented are corrupt, with nothing in the drama to indicate that this evil is deprecated. Besides the Jatra, there is usually a *nautch*, or dance, by the poor abandoned women who follow this profession.

All tends to corruption and materialism. Only outward rites, the invention of priestcraft, remain, with selfishness and superstition, without love, purity or holiness. The true "Light of Asia" is the Asiatic Nazarene, who will come to his own and give them light.

CHAPTER XIX.

PILGRIMAGES AND HOLY PLACES.

All over India you hear constantly of *Tirth,* Hindu pilgrimage; or *Hajiya,* Mohammedan pilgrimage; or a pilgrimage of the Parsees to the burning lakes, somewhere on the Caspian Sea, where they believe the god of fire has his home. There is also the pilgrimage of the Buddhist to Buddha's birthplace, besides almost innumerable minor shrines and sacred rivers, sacred trees, as the old stump of a banyan in the underground passage of the fort at Allahabad; old temples and special places dedicated to special gods, as Mutra, for those who especially revere Krishna. Tanjore, Madura and Tinnevelly receive the greatest throngs of Siva worshipers, and so on through the endless list of gods and goddesses, each having a special shrine, or city, to which long and fatiguing pilgrimages are made by devout Hindus, Parsees or Mohammedans. Southern India is the place where the greatest honor is paid to Siva. At the three cities mentioned, Tanjore, Madura and Tinnevelly, are to be found the finest temples in point of grandeur and size that have been erected to the worship of this god. Travelers consider the one at Tanjore as the first. It is inside an immense quadrangle, surrounded by a double row of cells, or cloisters, for the priests and "holy men." Midway on two sides of the enclosure are arranged one

283

hundred and eight black stone Lingas of different sizes, one for each of the principal names of Siva. Behind these are grotesque frescoes on the wall. This image, the *Linga,* is used in all temples devoted to Siva or "Maha-deva," or "Maha-deo"—*Maha* meaning "great," and *deva,* or *deo,* "god." This symbol represents the male generative organs, or, more frequently, those of both sexes. Inside the quadrangle there is a little grove of palm and other trees, and in the principal temple an innermost sanctuary of the sacred Linga. Strangers are not allowed to approach the temples in South India. In Benares, however, where such throngs of tourists resort, you may go very near even the most sacred spot. Outside this great temple at Tanjore is a gigantic statue of Siva's bull. This image is in an open hall of fine architecture.

Besides the Linga there are many images of other gods and goddesses in side temples, besides gods and their exploits pictured on the walls. This is one of the one thousand and eight temples of Siva to be found in India, besides thousands of shrines dedicated to him. To all these pilgrims come to worship, as will presently be described. In connection with the Benares temples Kali's temples are equally numerous. Kali is the dark, blood-thirsty wife of Siva. Durga is another manifestation of this wife, Parwati* another, and so on. At Madura, Minakshi, the wife of Siva, is really the popular deity of the district, according to great authorities on Indian deities. The festi-

*One of the principal temples of Parwati is at Poona. (Chap. IV.)

STONE HOG AT BARMON ON THE NARBUDDA RIVER.
See Chap. XVI.

FIGURE OF THE SACRED BULL IN THE TEMPLE OF
PARWATI, POONA.

vals held in her honor are coarse and debasing, and are called "oil-festivals." The idol is undressed, its head anointed with oil, redressed and decorated amid an incessant noise of shouting, singing, the beating of tom-toms and other deafening instruments. Lights are waved, cowries are thrown, while the procession, headed by the god Ganesha, moves along. Whatever the admirers of Hinduism may say about the theoretic beauties of this ancient and conglomerate religion, yet to a dweller in India it is plain that grossness and sensuality, combined with much inert fatalism, control the masses.

The temple of Ramesvara,* situated on an island nearly connecting India with Ceylon, is counted as second in sanctity to Benares. To first journey through Benares, go through more than a hundred ceremonies, pay large fees to the Brahmins, pour plenty of Ganges water on the Linga in the temples there, bathe in the Ganges and then take a jar of water to Ramesvara, toiling on foot, through sand and dust, for twelve hundred miles, will insure perfection of bliss in the life to come for ages and ages.

A traveler gives a touching incident which occurred at this place just before his arrival there: A father and son had, after months of suffering and hard travel, succeeded in reaching the other side of the channel and the temple was actually in sight, when the father died suddenly on the road, leaving the little

---

*For information regarding the great temples in South India, I am indebted to Sir Monier Williams and his book "Brahminism and Hinduism."

boy destitute. He had, however, his precious jar of water. With this he hurried on to the shrine. Not knowing how precious his burden was, the presiding priest closed the door in the child's face, because the little fellow had no fee to give him. The boy's outburst of grief was terrible. Ruled by the priests with a rod of iron, they find no love, no care, no sympathy in the caste and the ceremonies they so blindly worship.

The Siva temples have many legends connected with trees. In some places the mango tree, while in other places the vata tree, the jambu tree and others are woven into the stories about Siva. Serpent-worship is also connected with this god. At Jagan-nath— the great temple at Puri, in Orissa—one hundred thousand annually eat the sacred food which is distributed in the courts of the temple, for here caste is discarded for the time.

The rock-hewn temples at Ellora, or Ellora Caves, one of the wonders of the world, are considered very holy as well as ancient.

Leaving Siva temples and shrines we may notice a few of the other gods and goddesses and their shrines. At Gaya there is a large Vishnu temple where *sraddhas,* or prayers for the dead, are performed. These sraddhas may be made on the banks of pools, or streams—places consecrated by the footprints of Vishnu, as this temple at Gaya—or they may be offered in cowhouses. *Pindas* (balls of rice) and milk are placed with leaves of the tulsi plant in earthenware platters, then sprinkled over with flowers and kusa grass. The hands of the performers are

purified by holding kusa grass. Water is then poured into the palms and this is scattered over the pindas and the ground; threads from the clothes are added to typify presenting garments to the dead. Prayers and texts by the priests accompany all this. Finally, bowing the head to the feet of the Brahmin, the ceremony concludes with, of course, a fee to his highness the priest. Thousands flock to Trichinopoly, the wonderful sacred city inclosed in an inner and outer, with five middle walls. This contains jeweled images, many-storied towers rivaling the great rock of Trichinopoly in height, gateways and innumerable columns, and has cost millions of rupees and required years for building. Thousands of the priests make their living from the pilgrims. In the inner wall, leading to the most sacred shrine, is a door called "Heaven's Gate." The idol is carried inside, bedecked and ready to receive the gifts of the throngs. Amid deafening noises the crowd passes through Heaven's Gate. Do you see them? Some go from a vague sense of duty, some because their forefathers have done the same from time immemorial, but the most, doubtless, carrying the conviction that the passage of this earthly heaven's gate, opened by the priests at their bidding, will be a sure passport to Vishnu's heaven after death.

At all these temples there are troops of dancing-girls, married to the god, but really slaves to the licentious desires of the Brahmins, who belong to the temples or who visit there. The visions of the most enthusiastic theosophist, worshiper of Mahatmas, or ideal admirer of Hindu mysticism, would fade away before the awful realities witnessed in these holy places, these

worshiping throngs, and, above all, the scenes along the river's edge, all proclaim superstition, impurity, vileness—a people given over to uncleanness and all abominations.

We spent the most of our time in a boat going up and down the two miles of river front. The numerous ghäts are long flights of wide stone steps reaching down below the water's edge. All day long, and most of the night, these great steps are literally covered with throngs of people, all eager to wash away their sins by a plunge into Mother Ganges. As one after another comes down into the river, they lift their folded or outstretched hands, and, looking toward the far horizon, they breathe a prayer to the god of the waters. Some throw handfuls of water over their heads as they repeat their *mantras,* or prayers. The thought comes to us that this worship and these throngs have been repeated for hundreds, even thousands of years.

> "Oh! those generations old,
> Over whom no church-bell tolled!
> Sightless, lifting up blind eyes
> To the silence of the skies!
> For the innumerable dead
> Is my soul disquieted."

One of the ghäts is called the burning-ghät. Sitting in the boat we watched three or four bodies prepared for Hindu cremation. Whatever the rite of cremation may be elsewhere, here it partakes only of the repulsive. The bodies are brought on bamboo stretchers and are placed just inside the edge of the stream while the pyre is being made ready. This is

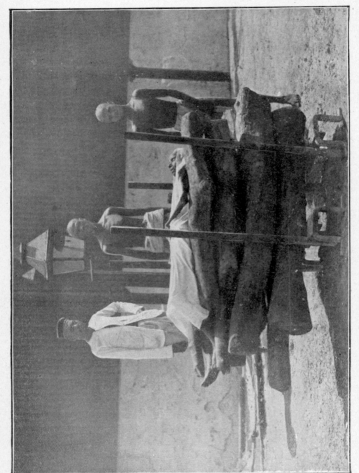

BURNING THE DEAD.

one of the places where suttee used to be performed before English law put a stop to the cruel practice. One corpse was that of a man of about forty years of age. His widow, in the white garments of widowhood, came down to the water's edge, and, dipping up some of the blessed Ganges, poured it over the face of the dead. When the body was lifted on to the pyre she helped to pile wood over it and it was her hand that applied the torch. When the sickening crackling began, and at a gesture from a relative—perhaps a command, for we were not near enough to hear—she picked up a stone, and, putting her hands alternately on the ground, she broke off the pretty glass bangles from her wrists and walked up the bank, a desolate widow, done with pleasures, ornaments and even respect, perhaps to endure treatment which will make her wish for the olden, sharper, but speedier death by suttee.

The dust of the burnings is strewn upon the beautiful stream, whose origin, according to Hindu mythology, is too revolting to mention. In the burnings much of the body is not reduced to ashes, owing to the very primitive arrangements. Near one of the pyres we saw a gaunt pariah dog gnawing away on the remains of a previous burning, and, on looking closely, we saw that his booty was a human skull. This, my first view of a burning-ghät, I hope may be my last.

Many strange and pathetic scenes were transpiring on all sides. The fakirs, or holy men, were to be seen everywhere—some at prayers, some in meditation and some bathing. A Brahmin priest was leading a young woman into the water. We were told that he was

giving her the holy bath. He dipped her up and down, mumbling incantations all the while. She placed the edge of his robe on her head at intervals, and the sad sight suggested temple-practices such as Pundita Ramabai tells us go on in this great city of Hinduism and elsewhere in India.

While we were still in the boat, an old ascetic died. We heard that he was to be immediately lowered into the river instead of being burned. This is a privilege of this class of men if they so desire. They tied large earthen pots to his arms and feet; then, rowing out into the stream a little way, while they blew an unearthly blast on a conch-shell, the disciples of the old devotee, laughing and chatting with apparent unconcern, tumbled the skeleton-like form overboard, and, turning the *chatties* so that they filled with water, the remains were soon out of sight beneath the flood.

In a garden near the monkey-temple we saw an old man—Shri Swami Bharkaranand Sarasvati by name—who is supposed by reason of his austerities to have attained to the state of deity. As we entered the garden in the chill of the early January morning we perceived the thin old man, on an upper veranda, in a state of nudity. He hastily donned a half yard of clothing—his robe of state, as it were, for he only puts it on for the reception of visitors—and came down the rose-bordered walk to meet us. To our surprise he took our hands in a friendly grasp. Then he presented us with a little book containing a short sketch of his life and the names of a long list of noted and unnoted foreign visitors who have come to see him.

He inquired all about us—our work, residence, and so on; then, bidding us to be sure to see his own marble image in a shrine on the other side of the garden, he smiled, salaamed and departed. *He did not ask us for bakshish,* and for that reason, if no other, we shall never forget Shri Swami, the holy man of Benares. We saw the life-size statue, done most exquisitely in pure white, glossy marble, with the eyes painted to exactly simulate life. People from far and near come to bow down and worship this saint's image.

We have seen Benares! To some extent we can comprehend the first clause in Isa. 57:5, and we can realize the necessity for some of the awful punishments meted out to idolaters in Bible times. We can give but a glimpse of Hinduism, with its multitudinous gods and its evil effects on mind, heart and body of man. The worst we see we dare not write, and we can never know the worst as it really exists. But in spite of all this dark picture, India is rising from the slough of superstition, for her light has come. Thousands of her idols have been crushed, and even into dark Benares the beneficent rays are piercing. Some day, not very distant, the ashes of the idols in this city shall strew the beauteous river, her inhabitants shall drink of the fountain of life and bathe, for cleansing, in the river of the water of life which proceedeth out of the throne of God and the Lamb.

There are many sacred spots on the banks of the rivers Narbudda and Jumna, besides Benares and other places on the Ganges, and even on smaller rivers, while sacred tanks are common. At Pushkar there is

a tank where sins are supposed to be cleansed away. At Allahabad there is held a great mela, or religious festival, at the junction of the Ganges and the Jumna. Here thousands of pilgrims resort every year. On the Narbudda, at Burman, a similar *mela* is held. This one is described in the chapter on "Up-country Scenes."

Another notable gathering is at Kumbaconam in South India, where, in a tank, "Mother Ganges" is supposed to appear from a subterranean passage once in twelve years. Several hundred thousand people congregate at this place at the time when the sacred waters appear. The priest stands in an elevated structure. The teeming thousands stand in the water, with hands outstretched or uplifted in prayer, waiting the signal of the priest to indicate that the Ganges has come. Then, with chants and prayers, the multitude plunges into the efficacious waters.

Could there be a sadder sight? Yes, a sadder one is the throng of returning, impoverished pilgrims— nothing wiser, nothing better, much poorer, but carrying away, as they will tell you, no joy, no peace, no sense of pardon. The great pilgrimage is over and no comfort has come to the soul, no new inspiration into the life. They have asked for bread, but a stone has been given them and they are starving still. They have looked for cleansing, but no sin has left them. They have looked for power, but none has come. They have bowed before hideous images, have recited texts and prayers, performed vigils and listened to stories of the gods—all in vain! With corrupt imag-

inations and perverted consciences, with foot-sore and aching bodies, they return as they came—unhelped.

Pilgrimages and holy places are not sufficiently noticed without a reference to the religious mendicants, the "holy men," or fakirs of India. Some admirers of Brahminism describe these men as ascetics who have renounced the world, the flesh and the devil and who give themselves up to the contemplation of God and spiritual matters. You have only to see these men to be satisfied that theirs is a kind of "holiness" that would not be tolerated in Christian lands. They travel from place to place, sometimes in bands of fifty or more, but more often singly. They beg or demand their living from the people, before whom they pose as devout men. They go nearly or quite naked, disfiguring their bodies with paint or ashes, and refrain from bathing, until, in that hot climate, their stench might announce their presence in the dark. Their hair is never cut, washed or combed, but is woven in a filthy basket-like mat about their heads, or hangs in stringy masses about their shoulders. Nearly all carry the dried outside cocoanut shell as a receptacle for gifts and alms. Their whole appearance is revolting and their minds and morals are as unclean as their bodies. These are the teachers in Hinduism and the same class abounds among Mohammedans.

Poor India!—seventy-three per cent of its people following after idols and are led by ignorant priests and disgusting sadhus, and the remaining twenty-three per cent submit to the sensual and treacherous teachings of the "false prophet" and his devotees, the fakirs! No living fountain of life from which to

quench her thirst; only the murky streams from the Vedas and Koran. When shall she be led into the beams from the Sun of Righteousness? Some day, neither at Benares nor at Mecca, but at a spiritual shrine of a spiritual God, shall all of India's wealth of devotion and self-sacrifice be poured. Old temples are crumbling, ancient faiths and superstitions fading away, and idols are being destroyed. Fairer than the dream-like Täj Mahal shall India's beauty shine forth, for in that day ashes and corruption shall give place to righteousness, purity and peace.

Dark India! stretching out helpless hands to those more favored.

> Christless, lifting up blind eyes
> To the silence of the skies!
> Still thy love, oh! Christ arisen,
> Yearns to save these souls in prison
> Through all depths of sin and loss
> Drops the plummet of thy cross!
> Never yet abyss was found
> Deeper than that cross can sound.

INDEX.

INDEX.

INDEX.

PRINTED BY R. R. DONNELLEY
AND SONS COMPANY, AT THE
LAKESIDE PRESS, CHICAGO, ILL.